"Lynn Anderson has captured the servant nature of biblical leadership. He accurately translates biblical models and prinicples of shepherding for churches in a cyber-world."

—C. Gene Wilkes, author *Jesus on Leadership*
and Senior Pastor Legacy Drive
Baptist Church, Plano, Texas

"I wholeheartedly recommend *They Smell Like Sheep*. It's a book for today's leader who wants to be effective now, tomorrow, next year, and into the next century. Anderson has once again skillfully turned us back to God's Word to discover critical answers for our future impact on the world."

—Jack Evans
former Mayor of Dallas, Texas

"At a time when churches desperately need to connect with their own as well as with the unchurched, Lynn Anderson provides illuminating insights into the biblical fundamentals of transforming service and leadership."

—Don Williams, Chairman
Trammell Crow Company

"Viewed as just another organization of people, the church over time has drifted into selection of its leaders based upon the same selection criteria utilized in corporate, industrial, and public service organizations. As a result, the church may be fiscally sound and efficiently reengineered, but spiritually bankrupt. With insight, clear examples, and very readable prose, Lynn Anderson reminds us of the kind of men and women the church needs in its leadership positions."

—R. Gerald Turner, President
Southern Methodist University

"*They Smell Like Sheep* holds up to church leaders the ideals of shepherding the flock with such a personal touch that all involved share the sweet aroma of Christ-likeness. Lynn Anderson supplies all spiritual leaders with the tools to appropriate the power of the Good Shepherd in their relationships with those they lead."

—Wilson C. Orr
Vice Chairman, Board of Trustees,
Abilene Christian University

"Few people can write a fine book on change management *(Navigating the Winds of Change)* and then write an equally good book on caring shepherding. Lynn Anderson can, which tells you why he's a minister I listen to and learn from."

—Kevin Miller, Editor
Leadership Journal

"Lynn's refreshing look at the functions and character of spiritual leaders fills a real need! He identifies 'what leaders do' as shepherds, mentors, and equippers of the people of God. And he explores the qualities of character which give them the moral influence to be effective shepherds. Very worthwhile!"

—Dr. Harold Hazelip, President
Lipscomb University

"I have had the opportunity to read much of what Lynn Anderson has written over the last ten years, and *They Smell Like Sheep* marks the start of a new era in Lynn's life and writing. It's not often one gets to say a book "smells," but this one does! It has the scent of wisdom, experience, authenticity and a heart for the church."

—Fred Smith, President
The Fourth Partner Foundation

"Just as Jesus is known for the disciples he mentored, so Lynn Anderson is known for those he has led—Max Lucado being just one outstanding example. In an age when most leaders are chosen for their managerial style, Lynn Anderson, in *They Smell Like Sheep,* provides a thoroughly biblical antidote to leadership styles that have pushed shepherding into the background and control into the foreground. The biblical model of 'shepherding' is making a comeback, and Anderson provides the biblical grounding we need to make it work."

—Leslie H. Stobbe, Dir. of Communications
Evangelistic Assoc. of New England

They Smell Like Sheep

They
Smell
Like
Sheep

Spiritual Leadership
for the 21st Century

DR. LYNN ANDERSON

HOWARD
PUBLISHING CO.
West Monroe, Louisiana

Our purpose at Howard Publishing is to:

- *Increase faith* in the hearts of growing Christians
- *Inspire holiness* in the lives of believers
- *Instill hope* in the hearts of struggling people everywhere

Because He's coming again!

They Smell Like Sheep
© 1997 by Dr. Lynn Anderson
All rights reserved

Published by Howard Publishing Co., Inc.,
3117 North 7th Street, West Monroe, LA 71291-2227

Printed in the United States of America

97 98 99 00 01 02 03 04 05 06   10 9 8 7 6 5 4 3 2

Library of congress Cataloging-in-Publication Data

Anderson, Lynn, 1936–
    They smell like sheep : biblical leadership for the 21st century / Lynn Anderson.
      p. cm.
    ISBN 1-878990-73-X (alk. paper)
    1. Christian leadership. 2. Pastoral theology I. Title.
    BV652.1.A526 1997
    253—dc21   97-3349
                                                                          CIP

Jacket Design by LinDee Loveland
Edited by Philis Boultinghouse

Scripture quotations not otherwise marked are from the New International Version,
© 1973, 1978, 1984 by International Bible Society. Used by permission Zondervan
Bible Publishers.

All italics in Scripture were added by the author for emphasis.

Dedicated
to
Lawrence Anderson—
my life-long shepherd,
my father,
my mentor and equipper

■

C O N T E N T S

■

PART ONE

A Biblical Look at Spiritual Leadership Principles:

The Sort of Things Leaders Do

PART TWO
A Biblical Look at Elders:
The Sort of People They Are

ACKNOWLEDGMENTS

This book has been forty years in the making. Hundreds of minds converge on its pages. Some are credited in text or endnotes. Some have long since fled my consciousness and their insights confused with my own. Thank you, whoever you are.

Most of the stories are about real people. Some are named with their permission. However, in most cases I have combined one story with another and/or assigned fictitious names and shuffled genders and data so that "similarities to persons living or dead" are purely coincidental.

Also, many people played midwife in the birthing of this book:

Twenty persons who evaluated the rough draft last summer.

Lyn Rose and Rene Heard who typed their fingers to the bone.

Philis Boultinghouse, of Howard Publishing Company. Your world-class editorial expertise and your cheerful patience under stress turned deadline drudgeries into joy. You are indeed a shepherd.

I am profoundly indebted to many shepherds from past trails:

From West Memphis, Arkansas—you shepherded Carolyn and me in the morning of our ministry. From Abilene, Texas—you helped "raise me" across my nineteen years as your preacher. From Dallas, Texas—my shepherds for the past five and a half years, and now partners with me in a new kind of ministry.

Special thanks to my soul brothers David Wray and David Lewis, consummate shepherds. We codiscovered shepherding, mentoring, and equipping during those golden years together. You both tower over me in more ways than one.

Finally, two more shepherds, most precious of all: my mother, Mary Anderson, gone to heaven these eight years and my father Lawrence Anderson—for decades shepherd of a church in Saskatchewan and my personal shepherd for a lifetime. Dad, you still walk the trail beside me even though we held a funeral in your honor more than six years ago. Thank you, Mom and Dad.

Finally, thank you Lord Jesus, my Chief Shepherd. Thank you sweet Holy Spirit. And thank you, Oh Yahweh, my heavenly father, my shepherd. You restore my soul. I *will* dwell in your house forever.

Stepping into the Pasture

Christian people everywhere are crying out for spiritual leaders—men and women grounded in the Word of God, made wise by the experiences of life, and filled with the love and compassion of Christ. As our culture spins faster and faster, churches are caught up in the whirlwind of change, and people sometimes get lost in the shuffle . . . like sheep without a shepherd.

If you are a *leader* or an *aspiring leader* of any kind, you can help fill the void. If you are an elder, deacon, minister, small group leader, worship leader, house church leader, Bible study leader, teen leader, a leader who brings lost people to Christ, a parent—even someone who *wants* to be a leader, read on. The simple, biblical principles laid out in this book will equip you with the skills you need to shepherd a flock and will help shape your heart into that of a shepherd who smells like sheep.

Shepherds Gone AWOL

Today's leaders face overwhelming expectations, yet are often hampered by unworkable systems. Some dash into the fray with lots of heart and too few skills—and get demolished. Others, with skills but no heart, leave behind them a trail of trouble. Still others, with both heart and skills, are hamstrung by antiquated ministry methods and leadership styles patterned after business models rather than after Jesus. Consequently, too many good leaders burn out or give up. Some even become adversarial and wind up with broken spirits and broken churches. Others plod on, but with little hope.

Recently, "Tom," one of the finest Christian men I know and the CEO of a multinational company, resigned as an elder of his church. And "Bill," a bright and dedicated minister, quit after fifteen years in ministry and is now working as a sales rep for a chain of discount stores. Both men, from different congregations, had given up hope of doing the real work of the church in the way Jesus would do it. Tom confided that one hour of the weekly elders' meeting was more stressful for him than ten hours in his business. Bill indicated that attempting to meet the unrealistic expectations of an entire congregation was simply taking too much of a toll on himself and his family. Neither Tom nor Bill felt they were making much positive difference.

Both men have discovered that leading a church is extremely tough in these days when values are vanishing, social norms are shifting, and families are falling apart. They have seen litigation lurking at the church doors, tensions between cultural and ethnic groups, inconsistent giving patterns, and conflict between traditional and progressive elements in the church. Their churches and families live fast-paced, urban life-styles, which seem to accelerate daily. Tom and Bill have learned the hard way that individualistic and consumer-minded church members often measure church leaders by a variety of competing and unrealistic standards.

Many other church leaders feel similar frustrations as they face calendars bulging with meetings, church events, counseling, trouble shooting, refereeing, and much more. Understandably, some leaders throw in the towel.

An Idea Whose Time Has Returned

In spite of leadership difficulties, a new spirit of hope and growth is moving through churches across the country. Good things are already underway, and the unfolding possibilities far outstrip any current problems. Armies of godly leaders are sensing the urgency of God's mission and the rapidly changing terrain of the playing field, and they are seeking both *heart* and *skills* to lead their churches into the twenty-first century in the way Jesus would want them to.

Even more significant, the Christian community at large is beginning to rediscover the biblical design for spiritual leadership—in the form of surprisingly simple and doable models. Briefly summarized, these models are *shepherding, mentoring,* and *equipping.* These simple principles not only offer promise of enormously improved effectiveness in changing lives, but they can lighten the burdens of current church leaders by spreading the spiritual nurturing burden across many more shoulders. Restoring and implementing these biblical spiritual leadership models is an idea whose time is returning.

The biblical model of spiritual leadership frees up church leaders to live in a glad new way for at least three reasons. First, because most Christians will *want* to follow real shepherds who mentor and equip them—shepherds whose lives are credible, whose relationships are authentic and warm, and whose ministry is genuine and helpful. Thus, the influence of this style of leader resides not in position or title but in respect and trust gained the old-fashioned way—by earning it!

Second, these leaders will live in a glad new way because a good deal of the shepherding *burden* will be lifted from their backs and spread across the shoulders of newly equipped shepherds who will join with them in simply putting their lives down beside a few people and leading them closer to Jesus.

Third, these leaders will live in a glad new way because they will see more *fruit* for their labors. Something wonderful is happening in our times as this biblical leadership model is being rediscovered by the body of Christ at large. The "divine alchemy" of the Spirit is turning thousands of sheep into shepherds; thus, the shepherding capabilities of the body of Christ are expanding exponentially.

A Shepherd Smells Like Sheep

Of the three biblical models, shepherd, mentor, and equipper, the chief model is that of *shepherd*—and with good reason, for a shepherd is someone who lives with sheep. A shepherd knows each sheep by name; he nurtures the young, bandages the wounded, cares for the weak, and protects them all. A shepherd *smells like sheep.*

In the body of Christ, we all play the role of shepherd to someone. You play the role of shepherd as you parent your child in the faith or teach a Sunday school class. You are a shepherd when you disciple a fellow Christian. Older men and women shepherd as they mentor younger men and women; you shepherd as you lead your small group or lead a friend to Christ. The biblical principles of shepherding are remarkably simple, yet powerfully impacting!

How This Book Can Help You Become a Godly Shepherd

This book is divided into two parts. Part 1 explores the implications of the three interrelated spiritual leadership models under the captions—*shepherd, mentor,* and *equipper.* These models help express God's leadership design in language that powerfully connects with the church in our time.

Part 2 focuses in on the biblical teaching about *elders* and the sort of people they are to be—people of *experience,* people of *character,* and people of *vision.* Then it moves into a discussion of the "authority" of *moral suasion* in a credible life based on service, relationships, and a consistent faith-walk.

They Smell Like Sheep goes out in the hope that it will stir more than a few godly men and women to dust off and revive God's design for spiritual leadership and bring fresh hope and fruitfulness to faithful shepherds across the Christian community. The concepts in this book have changed many lives, including mine, and have helped change the face of more than a few churches. Hopefully, they will refresh you and make glad the heart of the Chief Shepherd!

PART ONE

A Biblical Look at Spiritual Leadership Principles:

The Sort of Things Leaders Do

Section One:

Shepherds

Little Bo Peep has lost her sheep
and can't tell where to find them.
Leave them alone,
    and they'll come home,
wagging their tails behind them.

■

Suppose one of you has a
hundred sheep and loses one of
them. Does he not leave the
ninety-nine in the open country
and go after the lost sheep until
he finds it? And when he finds it,
he joyfully puts it on his shoulders
and goes home.

Luke 15:3–5

1

Shepherds on the Hills of Bible History

One Sunday, a dear friend and member of my congregation cornered me after a sermon in which I repeatedly referred to elders as "shepherds."

"Why don't you find a better way to communicate this spiritual leadership idea? No one in our church knows anything about shepherds and sheep—especially the way all that stuff worked in the ancient world. That picture just doesn't connect with a modern church."

Admittedly, the shepherd metaphor does sound strange in the cyber-world of our daily experience. We don't normally see these picturesque, rural characters rolling down the expressways or eating at our local McDonald's. But, after carefully considering my friend's suggestion and searching in vain for a contemporary metaphor that would better connect the biblical notion with our times, I finally had to explain, "I can't find any figure equivalent to the shepherd idea in our modern, urban world. Besides, if I drop the shepherd and flock idea, I would have to tear about five hundred pages out of my Bible, plus leave the modern church with a distorted—if not neutered—view of spiritual leadership." God keeps pointing shepherds to the pasture to struggle with sheep.

In Bible times, the shepherds were as common and familiar to most Middle Easterners as are telephones and supermarkets to modern-day Americans. Almost anywhere in the Bible world, eyes that lifted to gaze across the landscape would fall upon at least one flock of sheep. As my friend Ted Waller reminds us, in antiquity,

> the family often depended upon sheep for survival. A large part of their diet was milk and cheese. Occasionally, they ate the meat. Their clothing and tents were made of wool and skins. Their social position often depended upon the well-being of the flock, just as we depend upon jobs and businesses, cars and houses. Family honor might depend upon defending the flock.[1]

Shepherds throughout History

The shepherd metaphor shows up more than five hundred times in Scripture, across both Old and New Testaments. Without question, the dominant biblical model for spiritual leadership is the *shepherd* and *flock*. If we want to understand the biblical model for leadership, we must embrace the concept of shepherd.

God as Shepherd

In the "olden days" of the Old Testament world, the watch-care of God himself is pictured in the shepherd/sheep relationship. Most of us can quote the familiar words, "The Lord is my shepherd."[2] The prophet Isaiah penned this less familiar but equally eloquent picture of God, "He tends his flock like a shepherd: He gathers the lambs in his arms and carries them close to his heart; he gently leads those that have young."[3] What a winsome picture of our God!

Can't you just envision the awkward and delicate little lamb, ears askew, one gangly leg dangling near the shepherd's elbow? Notice that the shepherd tilts his head so that his beard nuzzles the lamb's cheek and his resonant voice murmurs gently to the lamb as they move through the twilight toward the rest and safety of the sheepfold. Old Testament readers would have pictured just such a gentle, caring relationship between God and his people—"the sheep of his pasture."[4] And although "we all, like sheep, have gone astray,"[5] we still have a "good shepherd" who will love us and lead us gently back to the fold.

Prophets, Priests, and Kings as Shepherds

Later, God pictured his prophets, priests, and kings as shepherds. When God chose David—the shepherd-*king* after God's "own heart"[6]—he "took him from the sheep pens; from tending the sheep he brought him to be the shepherd of his people. . . . And David shepherded them with *integrity of heart.*"[7]

God also expected the *prophets* and *priests* of Israel to shepherd his people, but they often failed miserably at their task. Although many did not live up to their role as shepherd, God came back again and again to the idea that the leaders of his people were *shepherds*—even though some were *bad* shepherds.

God warned these "false shepherds" in graphic language; and in no uncertain terms, he pronounced woes on their heads. The prophet Jeremiah blasted the "shepherds" of Judah for misleading their flock, setting it up for captivity in Babylon.

> My people have been lost sheep; their shepherds have led them astray and caused them to roam on the mountains. They wandered over mountain and hill and forgot their own resting place.[8]

Leaders who were responsible for the spiritual well-being of Judah shirked their duties and instead indulged their own selfish desires. The Lord's rebuke comes through loud and clear in this passage from Ezekiel:

> Woe to the shepherds of Israel who only take care of themselves! Should not shepherds take care of the flock? . . . You have not strengthened the weak or healed the sick or bound up the injured. You have not brought back the strays or searched for the lost. You have ruled them harshly and brutally. So they were scattered.[9]

Then he spells out their sentence:

> Weep and wail, you shepherds; roll in the dust, you leaders of the flock. For your time to be slaughtered has come; you will fall and be shattered like fine pottery.[10]

The shepherd metaphor for the leaders of Israel was not lost on the Israelite people. Those ancient folks knew that the food on their tables and the clothes on their backs—not to mention the family honor—was inexorably linked to the way they cared for their flocks. And thus, they understood that the very spiritual survival of their nation hinged on the quality of work done by their leaders.

It goes without saying that the prophetic warnings against the unfit spiritual shepherds of Israel hold implications for today's church leaders. Today's leaders carry life and death responsibility for their people, just as did the prophets, priests, and kings of old.

Jesus as Shepherd

■

In the New Testament, Jesus is our shepherd. In the Old Testament, God had dropped hints of the coming shepherd through the prophet Ezekiel: "I will place over them one shepherd, my servant David, and he will tend them . . . and be their shepherd. I the Lord will be their God, and my servant David will be prince among them."[11]

Speaking of himself as the loving shepherd, Jesus says that he leaves the ninety-nine in the open country and goes in search of the lost *one*. "And when he finds it, he joyfully *puts it on his shoulders* and goes home."[12] He drapes this stinky, wayward sheep around his neck and carries it home. Think of it. Jesus left the comforts of heaven and came into our universe, our pasture, to smell like sheep! Jesus sweated like we do. He walked our pathways, braved our wolves, faced our temptations, and shared our struggles. The Holy One of Israel came in Jesus Christ to be our good shepherd.

Can't you just envision the awkward and delicate little lamb, ears askew, one gangly leg dangling near the shepherd's elbow?

■

My friend Roy tells a fascinating story about a trip to Palestine some years back. One afternoon, he stood on a ridge overlooking a long, narrow gorge. Below him, the gorge opened out into rolling grass-covered pasture lands. A single trail meandered down the length of the gorge floor, then branched out into dozens of trails when it reached the grasslands. A group of shepherds strolled down the gorge trail, chatting with one another, followed by a long, winding river of sheep. At the forks of the trail, the shepherds shook hands and separated, each taking a different path as they headed out into the grasslands. Roy recounted the fascinating sight that followed.

■

Think of it. Jesus left the comforts of heaven and came into our universe, our pasture, to smell like sheep!

■

As the shepherds headed their separate ways, the mass of sheep streaming behind them automatically divided into smaller flocks, each flock stringing down the branch trail behind its appropriate shepherd. When the various shepherds and their flocks were distanced from each other by a few hundred yards, each shepherd turned to scan his own sheep, noting that some strays had been left behind and were wandering in confusion among the rocks and brush.

Then one of the shepherds cupped his hands around his mouth and called in a strange, piercing cry, "Ky-yia-yia-yia-yia." At his shout, a couple of stray lambs perked up their ears and bounded toward his voice. Then a second shepherd tilted back his head calling with a distinctly different sound, "Yip-yip-yip-yipoo-yip." A few more strays hurried straight toward him. Then another called his strays with a shrill, "Hoot-hoot-hoot!" Each shepherd, in turn, called. Each of the strays, hearing a familiar voice, knew exactly which shepherd he should run to. "In fact," my friend Roy marveled, "none of the wandering sheep seemed to notice any voice but the voice of his own shepherd."

This is what Jesus meant when he said, "My sheep listen to my voice," but "do not recognize a stranger's voice."[13] The sheep pick his voice out of a cacophony of voices and follow it. The shepherd "calls his own sheep by name and leads them out. When he has brought out all his own, he goes on ahead of them, and his sheep follow him because they know his voice."[14]

This is the essence of spiritual leadership: sheep following a shepherd because they know and trust him. This kind of trust and allegiance can be gained only one way—by a shepherd touching his sheep, carrying them, handling them, tending them, feeding them—to the extent that he *smells* like them.

When the apostle Peter instructed church leaders on how to lead, he spoke of Jesus as "the Chief Shepherd."[15] We must not miss Peter's point. Jesus, the Chief Shepherd is our model: he is the archetype, the blueprint, for the way modern, Christian leadership gets done.

Even contemporary believers instinctively warm to Jesus' comforting words of sheep and shepherding. Because Jesus laid his life down for us, he woos us and wins our trust, our affection, and our loyalty.

Good spiritual shepherds today imitate the Chief Shepherd. Like him, they attract flocks through loving service and authentic relationships. Like him, they feed and protect their flocks. They know their flocks and their flocks know them. They are trusted as men and women who are committed enough to put their lives on the line, daily, for the precious people they lead.

The Apostles as Shepherds

After modeling shepherd leadership, Jesus passed the model on to the apostles. Three times in one brief conversation, Jesus charged Peter (possibly as a representative of the entire apostolate):

"Feed my lambs,"[16] "Take care of my sheep,"[17] and "Feed my sheep."[18] By implication he is saying, "Adopt my spiritual leadership style."

Later, he told the Father, "As you sent me into the world, I have sent them."[19] One would find it hard to believe that after three years of watching Jesus and being coached by him—and now commissioned by him—that these twelve men would invent new leadership strategies. Jesus had modeled the shepherd style of leadership, and this is what they used in their lives and modeled to others.

Today's Leaders as Shepherds

Both Peter and Paul passed the shepherd model of leadership on to us. Paul pleaded with the leaders of the church in Ephesus,

> Keep watch over yourselves and all the flock of which the Holy Spirit has made you overseers. Be *shepherds* of the church of God, which he bought with his own blood.[20]

Again Peter wrote,

> Be shepherds of God's flock that is under your care . . . eager to serve; not lording it over those entrusted to you, but being examples to the flock. And when the *Chief Shepherd* appears, you will receive the crown of glory that will never fade away.[21]

Let me grab the modern church leader by the literary ears: this shepherd metaphor was passed on to us intentionally! By the time Paul and Peter call church leaders "shepherds," the shepherd motif had gathered centuries of significance. A massive iceberg of divine meaning had accumulated across the Bible and now lay below the surface of this word. Peter and Paul are invoking a whole theology of spiritual leadership, not merely throwing in a colorful figure of speech.

So I told my modern friend, who had trouble with ancient shepherds, "I guess I'll stick with the shepherd idea. Seems better to try and help us both understand what the shepherd model is about than to butcher my Bible and run the risk of distorting God's plan."

This metaphor and its implications are worth pondering. No question: some spade work lies ahead of those who unearth this pastoral, rural metaphor and connect it with our hi-tech, urban experience; however, a little digging is well worth the effort because what we uncover is indispensable to a clear, biblical understanding of spiritual leadership.

The Relational Basis of Shepherding

The Biblical Shepherd

While some may not feel comfortable thinking of certain people as sheep and others as shepherds, our discomfort will likely disappear when we realize that the shepherding model revolves around the *relationship* between the shepherd and his flock. It is not a figure of strong over weak or "lords" over servants. Quite the contrary. The shepherd figure is one of love, service, and openness.

Ancient, Middle-Eastern shepherds lived in the pasture with the flock and were as much a part of the land as the sheep were. Through a lifetime of shared experience, shepherds nurtured enduring trust relationships with their sheep.

When a tiny lamb was born into the wilderness world, the shepherd took the trembling newborn into his hands, warming it and caressing it. Among the first sensations felt by the shivering lamb was the tender hands of the shepherd. The gentle voice of the shepherd was one of the first sounds to awaken the lamb's delicate eardrums.

The shepherd lived with the lambs for their entire lives—protecting them, caressing them, feeding and watering them, and leading them to the freshest pools and the most luxuriant pastures—day and night, year in and year out. So by the time the lamb grew to "ewe-hood" or "ram-hood," it naturally associated the touch of the shepherd's hands and the sound of the shepherd's voice with "green pastures" and "still waters," with safety, security, love, and trust. Each sheep came to rely on the shepherd and to know his voice and his alone. They followed him and no one else.

Of course, the lambs understood clearly who was in charge. Occasionally, the shepherd might tap an unruly lamb on the ear with a shepherd's crook. But this was a love tap, embraced in an enfolding circle of relationship. The shepherd smelled like sheep!

When the day's grazing was done and night was approaching, the shepherd would gather the sheep together and lead them into a protective fold. Some were crude, makeshift circles of brush, stick, and rocks, forming barricades four or five feet high—safe little fortresses in the wilderness. Others were limestone caves in the hillsides. Even today, in Palestine, one can see roughly constructed, temporary sheepfolds dotting the pastoral landscape. But each circle is incomplete, broken at one place to form an opening into the fold. Beside this portal the shepherd would take his place as he gathered his flock into the fold for the night, at times physically becoming the "gate."[22]

Part of the nighttime ritual was the gentle inspection of each, individual lamb. One by one, each lamb would come under the shepherd's rod for review. Each would feel the shepherd's hands and hear his voice speaking its name. Under the care of the shepherd, the sheep would "come in and go out, and find pasture."[23]

"Good evening my friend, Yellow-Wool. You look tired. Long day? C'mon inside and rest. And you, Ragged-Ear, let me pull that tick from your cheek. Come in, Spotted-Face, Broken-Foot, Shiny-Nose . . . " until all the sheep were snuggled inside the safety of the fold for another night.

With the whole flock examined and bedded down, finally, the shepherd himself would lie down, stretching his body across the opening. So, the shepherd literally, physically *became the door!* His body kept the sheep in and the dangers of the night out. No sheep could wander into danger because the shepherd's body held them in. Wolves and robbers could enter to harm the flock only over the dead body of the shepherd. Some claim that, even in modern times, morning will occasionally find scattered sheep, without a shepherd. Upon investigation, a bleeding, battle-worn shepherd will often be found somewhere nearby—sometimes even a dead one. The shepherd would literally lay "down his life for the sheep."[24]

■

Among the first sensations felt by the shivering lamb was the tender hands of the shepherd.

■

What a compelling and fitting model for leadership. No wonder the shepherd metaphor is a constant theme of the Bible. And along with the other two models we'll look at—mentor and equipper—its root is in *relationship* and its model is Jesus.

The Contemporary Shepherd

Grab your pencil. Get ready to circle the next profound phrase. *A shepherd is someone who has a flock.* As obvious as that may sound, it is frequently overlooked—for many church "leaders" function in name or office only and in reality have no flock.

Flocks naturally gather around food, protection, affection, touch, and voice. Biblical shepherds are those who live among the sheep; serve the sheep; feed, water, and protect the sheep; touch and talk to the sheep—even lay down their lives for the sheep. Biblical shepherds *smell* like sheep.

■

A shepherd is someone who has a flock!

■

One shepherdess who smells like sheep is my wife Carolyn. Carolyn frequently "adopts" lonely young singles who move to our area. "Tim" was one of them. Our circle of friends loved Tim for his fun personality and his servant heart. We all quickly became very attached to him. Eventually, Tim confided to Carolyn and me that he had a serious, life-threatening illness. As the illness progressed, he and Carolyn became especially close. She spent countless hours with him in his final weeks—often just hugging and holding him like her own child. Outside of his own loving family, she was one of the very last to touch Tim before he died. The following note from Carolyn was read at Tim's funeral.

My friend, Sunday, when I kissed you on the forehead, you looked into my eyes and said, "Thank you."

But it is I who should thank you. Thank you for the way I saw your life grow in Christ. Thank you for sharing a day last year helping me decorate my Christmas tree. Thank you for the blackberry cobbler on my birthday. Thank you for the Weatherford peaches you brought by early one morning. Thank you for asking that I be present when the elders called a special meeting to pray for your healing.

Today, I celebrate, and I ask everyone who loved you to celebrate with me.

This was true shepherding by a lady who touches her flock personally and deeply and is touched by them as well.

Church leaders who shepherd well will foster congregational infrastructures that leave them plenty of time and opportunity for flock-building. A good deal of their leadership will be hands-on and personal—for this is how flocks are formed.

The shepherd and flock relationship eloquently implies at least three qualities of spiritual leadership: *availability, commitment,* and *trust.* This is how spiritual flocks are formed today.

Relationships Require Availability

Two of my warmest memories of "available" shepherds find Wally Bullington walking around in them. Wally was a football coach; he is now retired, but is still known by most people as "coach." Wally shoots straight, but always with love and warmth and follow-through.

One memory comes from a church-wide father/child canoe trip on the Guadelupe River. Two kids came along who had no dad at home. Wally spent hours with them—teaching them to tie flies, paddle canoes, catch fish, set up tents, and more.

> Jesus talked with them until they began to hear his voice way down in their souls.

The other memory involves the son of a single-parent mother. When this young boy's parents were accused of a crime, he felt socially cut off from everyone. In addition, it appeared that he might have to drop out of his much-loved private school.

Many afternoons found Wally throwing a football with this boy on a vacant lot.

Years later, both boys, now men, still see Wally as a father figure and stay in touch with him for counsel and love. He touched many others as well. Shepherd Wally built long relationships with these lambs and earned their trust, affection, and loyalty. Because he made himself accessible and available, these sheep know Wally's voice and follow him. Authentic, spiritual bonding like this is as real as family blood ties—maybe more so—and in some ways, just as irreplaceable. Around this shepherd, a flock gathered across the years—a flock that authentically loves him, depends on him, follows him, and listens to his voice.

Relationships Require Commitment

Shepherding sheep requires a long-term, costly commitment of self, time, and energy and the building of open, authentic relationships. Shepherding is no easy task. Jesus, the "Chief Shepherd," exemplified this commitment in his relationship with the Twelve. Jesus chose them so that "they might be *with* him,"[25] and for three years, they went everywhere he went. They went with him to weddings, temples, villages, fields, synagogues, and sickrooms. They even went fishing together. Jesus changed them by his touch. He taught them, ate with them, and protected them. He talked with them until they began to hear his voice way down in their souls. Eventually, people could tell by being around them that "they had been with Jesus."

Modern-day shepherds rarely have the opportunity to spend such constant time with their sheep; but the intentionality of Christ, his relational approach, his commitment—these we can emulate.

Jim is absolutely unavailable on Wednesday nights to anyone outside room 222. Why? Because he has committed this time to a Challenge group led by Dr. Jan Dunn, which gathers in that room. Challenge is a special group hosted by our church. It began as a divorce recovery group, then broadened to include any persons struggling with painful relationships, whether divorced, married, or single.

At first, Jim went to encourage Jan. Jan is an experienced professor and practitioner of marriage and family therapy, but she felt unsure about whether her efforts would be affirmed by the church or whether they would even help people. Jim committed his Wednesday evenings, for an entire year, to being an affirming presence to the Challenge group—and the group has flourished! Over this past year, many have found recovery and healing—and God. Jim's role is low profile; he rarely says anything except when requested to lay hands on some specific anguishing person and pray for him or her. However, his shepherding presence has legitimated the whole effort. One in the group said, "Gosh. Just the nonjudgmental, compassionate presence of an elder in the room is as healing as anything else the class offers." Jim gets sheep smell all over himself on Wednesday nights, and he loves it. Jim definitely has "gathered a flock."

Relationships Require Trust

Sheep follow their shepherd "because they know his voice."[26] Through hours and days and weeks and years spent with their shepherd, sheep come to know from experience that they can trust him. Trust is *earned,* not demanded, and it is built *over time.*

We trust Jesus because he keeps his promise to be *with* us to the end of the world.[27] When we first come to him as trembling, newborn lambs, he caresses us in his gentle, firm hands. His love warms us, protects us, and feeds us. His spirit waters us, and he continually talks to us. He never abandons us or misleads us. We trust him because he is *trustworthy*.

So it is with modern-day shepherds. Men and women who would lead a flock must earn the trust of the sheep. When the lives of leaders are invested in the lives of sheep, the sheep come to know and trust their voices. This is what Jesus meant when he said that a shepherd's sheep "follow him because they know his voice."

Not only do the sheep know the shepherd, but the shepherd also knows the sheep—intimately. "He calls his own sheep by name." 28 Biblical leaders know faces and names—and personal stories. Because the shepherd knows and serves them all, they trust him, and he "leads them out." 29

Being placed in a leadership position does not guarantee a following, but a trail of sheep will usually follow the voice of a trusted shepherd.

Jack was successful in business, visible in the community, had been a deacon for years, and was loved by many people. But friends saw alcohol sneak up on him, until his world began to unravel—business, health, family. Finally, through an intervention initiated by my wife, Carolyn, Jack checked into a treatment center. Now aided by a twelve-step group, Jack has been sober for more than eight years. Throughout the process, Jack gained a whole new vision of God and a life of flourishing relationships.

Back on the fifth anniversary of his sobriety, the shepherds of Jack's church threw a huge "dinner party/sobriety celebration."

> ■
>
> When the lives of leaders are invested in the lives of sheep, the sheep come to know and trust their voices.
>
> ■

This did wonders for Jack and his family. And the positive shepherding implications spread out from that gesture—like circles from a rock thrown into a pond—reaching the far corners of their 2,000-member church and beyond. That one evening instilled hope and inspired trust in those shepherds on the part of many more Christians who were struggling with alcohol addictions. Acceptance and healing flowed through one key shepherding act.

In a society where trust is rarely extended or deserved, the "shepherd" style of leadership—by its very nature—*inspires trust.* God's design fosters trust in church leaders and nurtures loyalty between church members.

Even after this brief look at the biblical metaphor of shepherd, it's easy to understand why God chose such a model for spiritual leadership. Its implications are as applicable today as they were two thousand years ago. When godly, loving, gentle shepherds first build authentic relationships with their flocks, then rise up and "lead out," sheep hungry for biblical leadership and wise guidance will willingly follow.

■

You must decide
whether or not you
will design your life
after the pattern of
Jesus, or design your
life around the best
thinking the world has
to offer.

C. Gene Wilkes

CHAPTER

2

Distorted Leadership Models

Several years ago in Palestine, Carolyn and I rode a tour bus through Israel's countryside nearly mesmerized as the tour guide explained the scenery, the history, and the lifestyle. In his description, he included a heart-warming portrayal of the ancient shepherd/sheep relationship. He expounded on how the shepherd builds a relationship with his sheep—how he feeds them and gently cares for them. He pointed out that the shepherd doesn't drive the sheep but leads them, and that the shepherd does not need to be harsh with them, because they hear his voice and follow. And so on . . .

He then explained how on a previous tour things had backfired for him as he was giving this same speech about sheep and shepherds. In the midst of spinning his pastoral tale, he suddenly realized he had lost his audience. They were all staring out the bus window at a guy *chasing* a "herd" of sheep. He was throwing rocks at them, whacking them with sticks, and siccing the sheep dog on them. The sheep-driving man in the field had torpedoed the guide's enchanting narrative.

The guide told us that he had been so agitated that he jumped off the bus, ran into the field, and accosted the man, "Do you understand what you have just done to me?" he asked. "I was spinning a charming story about the gentle ways of shepherds, and here you are mistreating, hazing, and assaulting these sheep! What is going on?"

■

> The guy was chasing a "herd" of sheep. He was throwing rocks at them and whacking them with sticks.

■

For a moment, a bewildered look froze on the face of the poor sheep-chaser, then the light dawned and he blurted out, "Man. You've got me all wrong. I'm not a shepherd. I'm a *butcher!*"

This poor, unwitting fellow had just provided the tour guide and all of us with a perfect example of what a "good shepherd" is not.

Several distorted leadership models find their way into modern-day churches. They pop up in discussions about leadership, distorting perceptions of biblical shepherding and confusing sincere church members. Of course, these distorted models are not really welcome, but they hang around anyway. Most church members are not even conscious of their presence. Yet many churches seem to have a love/hate relationship with them, even a codependency.

Who are these guys, anyway?

Hired Hand

Jesus, in John 10, exposes our first distorted leadership model—the hired hand.

> The hired hand is not the shepherd who owns the sheep. So when he sees the wolf coming, he abandons the sheep and runs away. Then the wolf attacks the flock and scatters it. The man runs away because he is a hired hand and cares nothing for the sheep.[1]

Back in ancient times, shepherding was not a part-time, fair-weather affair. Shepherds did not get their jobs by dressing up, splashing on some "rugged" cologne, and answering an ad in the newspaper: "Help wanted on sheep ranch in remote rural area."

"Do you have any experience herding sheep?"

"Not really."

"No problem. There's an orientation course this afternoon from one to four."

Jesus, who enters by the gate, stands in stark contrast to this "hired hand," who apparently works only for a paycheck and cares nothing for the sheep. The hired man, Jesus said, runs away when things get difficult.

Modern-day hirelings are the kind of leaders who abandon the sheep to save themselves. Some hireling "church leaders" desire the leadership position only to garner power or visibility for themselves, but when the role requires time-consuming counseling or elicits uncomfortable criticism, they "abandon the sheep and run away." Others, under pressure, do the "organizationally expedient" thing in order to personally dodge the wolves and save their own reputational skin, and in so doing, leave the flock vulnerable and scattered.

Cowboy

Another distorted model is that of *cowboy.* Some people in leadership roles confuse shepherds and cowboys, but the difference is elementary—shepherds lead; cowboys drive. All of us have watched dusty westerns in which cowboys drive the herd by shouting, cracking whips, or stinging the stubborn cattle with sticks and prods.

> ■
>
> The difference is elementary —shepherds lead; cowboys drive.
>
> ■

But Jesus did not describe himself as "the brave cowboy"; rather, he described himself as "the Good Shepherd." Cowboys wear spurs, ride cutting horses, crack whips, and wield prods. Cowboys *force* the "herd" to go their way.

Not so the shepherd. The shepherd depends upon relationship. Jesus *leads* us in paths of righteousness—where we fear no evil and where our cups run over, even in "the valley of the shadow of death."[2] And Jesus does not expect his sheep to go where he has not gone. His challenge is not that we strike out on our own in unknown territory, but that we follow him: "If anyone would come after me, he must deny himself and take up his cross and follow me."[3]

Admittedly, in modern-day America or New Zealand, shepherds may attempt cowboy tactics with their sheep; but not so the ancient shepherds. Ancient shepherds *led* the flock.

Sheriff

A close kin to the cowboy is the sheriff. This distorted model flashes a badge and brandishes a gun. He says he wants to enforce the law and keep the peace, and he "don't take nuthin' off nobody." He's the law, and what he says goes. He doesn't ask if you like it; he just demands that you do as he says.

Such leaders cannot expect the love, affection, and loyalty of "a following." They sometimes resort to *coercion* in order to get *cooperation,* but in reality, they get mere *compliance,* at best, and *rebellion,* at worst.

My friend Jim recalls an incident where a sheriff flashed his badge at his church. Seems that one of the elders at his church became embroiled in a quarrel with a charismatic and financially well-to-do deacon over some recent decision. One Sunday evening, as the two men walked across the parking lot in heated argument, the elder glared at the deacon and demanded, "Do you believe in the authority of the elders or not?" Jim said this actually meant, "Are you going to do what I say, or are you going to continue to talk?"

In another scenario, a picture appeared in the *Arkansas Democrat* some years back of an elder and a deacon on the steps of a metropolitan church building physically struggling with one another over some church documents. Hardly the touch of a gentle shepherd with one of his flock!

> ■
>
> The "sheriff" model tries to enforce the law and keep the peace, and he "don't take nuthin' off nobody."
>
> ■

Jesus warned the apostles against this distorted leadership model: "The rulers of the Gentiles lord it over them, and their high officials exercise authority over them. Not so with you."[4] The "lording over" leadership style is of the world and has no place in spiritual leaders. As my father used to say, "A church leader who has to *assert* his authority doesn't have much." Most parents realize that when they resort to the words, "Because I said so," they have already lost this relational round with their child.

Pop-Manager

There is no question that time constraint is a fierce enemy of modern-day spiritual shepherds, and some contemporary shepherds may be tempted to look for leadership models in pop-management shortcuts. But at all cost, fast-lane shepherds must resist the temptation to draw their modus operandi from the now-dated management models of the business world. Biblical leaders are spiritual shepherds, not one-minute managers, managing at the "speed of change."

CEO/Chairman of the Board

While few shepherd-hearted leaders would militantly defend the "distant CEO" view of leadership, some fall into it by benign neglect of shepherding opportunities. Type-A personalities are particularly prone to this thinking. They often regard fellowship events, small groups, and in-depth personal discussions as "fluff" or "touchy-feely" stuff—which, like quiche, is not palatable to "real men."

This thinking not only represents a profound misunderstanding of their role and its process, but sends fuzzy signals to the flock. Even when the sheep cannot consciously put their fingers on the specific problem, they feel a sense of loss when leaders neglect opportunities for informal contact with their people.

Not long ago I was privileged to attend an annual all-church picnic at a lovely lakeside retreat. The turnout was tremendous and the weather gorgeous. All ages spent the day chatting, playing table games, swimming, boating, playing volleyball, basketball, ping pong, etc. We ate together and celebrated like a huge, warm family. I found myself falling into no less than a dozen in-depth, personal conversations—about spiritual matters. But a cloud hung over the horizon: even though the event was described by a pair of godly deacons as something that moved the church a year down the road in one day, only one of that congregation's numerous elders showed up for this mega-opportunity to shepherd! "Conflicting schedules," some rationalized, but in so saying, they under-scored the low priority they put on shep-herding. In fact, those leaders missed an excellent pastoral opportunity and lost some prime-time flock building. The flock felt the loss and said so.

The distorted CEO model works mostly behind closed, boardroom doors—making decisions, tapping gavels, dispatch-ing memos, and announcing edicts: "It's policy. And that's that!"

Martin, a minister friend, recalls a boardroom-style interview he once walked through with a church. The interview process began as Martin was handed a copy of the church's personnel policy—a docu-ment several pages long. Each point of dis-cussion was divided into various sections and subsections (Section 8, Article 2, etc.).

■

The CEO model works mostly behind closed, boardroom doors—making decisions, tapping gavels, dispatching memos, and announcing edicts.

■

"I found it interesting," Martin observed, "that before these church leaders even knew whether or not I read the Bible, prayed, or loved my wife, they wanted to know if I could live with their personnel policy."

The proof that the CEO model doesn't work is in the absence of a following, for this kind of leader has no flock. No one comes to such leaders for shepherding, and the troubled and timid know to avoid them. Their voices are not heard because no one is listening. As Jesus said, sheep "will never follow a stranger; in fact, they will run away from him because they do not recognize a stranger's voice."[5]

Distorted models of leadership are sometimes decades old and deeply ingrained. And some good people, conditioned by old, secular styles, find the biblical shepherd model difficult to accept. Recently, after I had described the concept of "shepherding" to a group of leaders at a leadership retreat, an elder leader with advanced degrees in management and a retiree from a military career accosted me over coffee, "This fancy idea may all be well and good, but . . ."

At this point, he was interrupted (and I was rescued) by a shepherd-hearted fellow leader who reminded his colleague, "'Butt' is the language of goats, not of shepherds!" Nuff said.

God has provided a guide for spiritual leadership through his Word, and we must not allow our thinking to be shaped by traditional religious polity, prevailing management fads, nor by any other humanly conceived model. God has designed a model—revealed through Scripture, embodied in Jesus Christ, and passed on to spiritual leaders of all time. The model is embedded in the very name "pastor." When today's church leaders follow the shepherding style of nurturing and leadership, they reflect the very heart of God and imitate the ways of Jesus.

■

In too many churches
today, head tables
have replaced towels
and wash basins as
symbols of leadership
among God's
people.

C. Gene Wilkes

CHAPTER

Fast-Lane Flocks and Cyber-World Shepherds

Harold's lip quivered slightly as he wrung his napkin. He wore a gracious attempt at a smile, but his eyes revealed weariness and a bit of pain.

"'Shepherd' is a beautiful idea," he began, "Looks to me like that is what God wants of me as an elder in this church. But I am feeling at a total loss. How do I actually make this happen in the real world? Why, the first three days last week I was in New York to close a contract. Then I was back in the office for two more marathon days fighting paper wars. My desk wasn't even clean till I headed for Houston to inspect a plant there. I hit the deck by 5 A.M. and run all day. Maybe last week was worse than usual, but not much. And I'm not alone. The rest of the elders in my church find life fast-paced too.

"What's more, most of our congregation runs the same fast-track—young mothers, graduate students, sales managers, CEOs, attorneys, and single parents forced to work two jobs. The list runs on and on. How is a shepherd to do his thing? How do you get sheep smell on you when you don't touch them—except for a handshake and some quick words in the aisle Sunday morning, a quick phone call, or a cold, impersonal fax."

> ■
> "How do you get sheep smell on you when you don't touch them—except for a handshake and some quick words in the aisle Sunday morning?"
> ■

Ah yes. Harold and his flock live in the express lane of a cyber-world rather than a serene pasture—and yet, he longs to be a biblical shepherd. Can it happen? Yes, it can—but it's not easy, and it requires intentionality.

Of course, there is no simple plan that will work for all cyber-world shepherds; yet, we must not, cannot, allow the culture to swallow up the designs of God. Indeed, some elders I know are coming up with creative ways to shepherd fast-lane flocks.

Don, for example, touches his flock of four, high-powered Texas business and professional men who read through a designated short book of the Bible on their own each day for a week. Then they meet at 5 A.M. on Saturdays, before racquetball, to discuss practical *so what's?* for their lives.

John, a busy elder, has tapped in on a gold mine of devotional and learning time that his sheep spend aboard airplanes and in hotel rooms. He collects articles and copies them for his friends to take with them as "road reading" and to inspire journaling. Then he circles his flock twice a month for breakfast and sharing. He says it has moved his shepherding quotient up several levels.

Another shepherd, Charles, retreats with his flock of graduate students once a month for solitude and silence and to share thought-provoking discussion. Recently, for example, after a Saturday breakfast, they watched the movie on Francis of Assisi, *Brother Sun and Sister Moon,* and then spent half the day reflecting on its implications for their lives.

Shepherd Gene's flock of executives mutually agreed to read Scripture, reflect, and keep a daily spiritual journal, meeting periodically for a discussion and prayer breakfast. Each week, however, they connect by conference call, from all over the nation, for thirty minutes of conversation, prayer, and accountability, rotating the cost of the call among the group members.

Several shepherds I know swap weekly faxes of a quasi-accountability tone and, thus, shepherd one another.

Chris leads an e-mail flock—sharing questions and answers, prayers requests, spiritual counsel, and devotional tidbits on their daily electronic roundtable.

The list goes on of ways to stretch shepherding across time-crunches. Some skilled, pressure-cooker shepherds seize events that bring several people together in one spot as magic shepherding moments. In those magic moments, several sheep can be "touched" at once, *inside* the circle, while at the same time, shepherd-hearted signals get sent to the many *outside* the gathering. Some examples:

One Monday evening I watched our shepherds "tending flock" through two mighty, but graceful, acts of shepherding. Both of these acts fit into the time constraints of a hectic, urban fast-track world, yet personally, powerfully, and deeply touched the sheep.

First up, one Monday evening these elders drew the Carter family—Barry, Jana, Nathan, and Cameron—into the "shepherds' circle" to pray for little Cameron, a precious, bright-eyed, four-month-old girl born with serious congenital heart problems. Three days before her surgery was scheduled, our shepherds gathered round the Carter family, laid their shepherds hands on them, and spoke loving concern for the family—and for baby Cameron.

One shepherd voiced a stirring prayer for peace upon Barry, Jana, and Nathan. Another shepherd took little Cameron's face in his shepherd hands and, with trembling voice, spoke a blessing on her and prayed God's healing touch. Then our elders overwhelmed the Carters with tears and hugs. Powerful shepherding! And praise God, Cameron's surgery was swift and successful, and she is now a healthy, growing girl. In addition, long after Cameron's full recovery, the Carter family will feel those hands and hear those voices—maybe for a lifetime! Yet, it all happened in just a few warm and well-spent moments.

■

"We church people sometimes get so 'respectable' that hurting people can't stand to be around us."

■

That same evening, Dr. Jan Dunn and some friends from the high-demand jobs in the fast lane, brought the shepherds' circle an update on Challenge, the support group mentioned in an earlier chapter. Our elders' eyes glowed as Jan and the rest reported how God had touched hurting people through Challenge—Christian and nonbeliever alike. They told of divorced people who had found recovery (three sat right there in the circle), and troubled marriages that had found healing and skills for rebuilding. They shared how all had found a safe place and love. Then our shepherds poured out admiration for Jan and her Challenge team. They roundly endorsed the Challenge ministry and the people it brings our way. One shepherd said, "You folks are simply being Jesus Christ. Jesus spent most of his time loving the crushed and broken. We church people sometimes get so 'respectable' that hurting people can't stand to be around us. Thank God for you."

This lit up the faces of the Challenge group and out tumbled words of gratitude for the encouragement. Then more prayers ascended. Our shepherds walked from that room smelling like sheep. Their flock left feeling deeply cared for and with new tomorrows written across their faces. This is just one small sample of what shepherds can do. Yet all this transpired in less than forty-five minutes.

As we close, we return to Harold, whom we met at the top of this chapter. Harold has discovered that even brief "aisle meetings" (this is what he calls short, but personal, meaningful, and intentional conversations in the aisle after church services) can become valuable shepherding opportunities. Once he saw them as such, he gave them focus and intentionality and repeated them week after week for maximum benefit. Harold's conference calls, faxes, and e-mail are not ideal, of course; nevertheless, in our cyber-world, they are becoming a new way to "reach out and touch someone."

Harold says, "They are the *third* best thing to being there."

The impersonality of cyber-world technology definitely presents huge downsides, but this new technology can be a "rod and staff" in the hands of a thoughtful shepherd who uses it intentionally.

Shepherding in the fast-lane cyber-world is not easy, but a lot of busy shepherds are discovering that it *can* be done.

Section Two:

Mentors

A leader who develops
people, adds. A leader
who develops leaders,
multiplies.

John Maxwell

4

Those Who Have Walked a Long Time in the Same Direction

Ted moves and looks like an athlete. He is usually confident and assertive, but today, sitting in front of the counselor, he seems almost fragile. Ted is a new Christian and the father of two children, ages four and seven. And Ted has hit a wall.

"I don't really know what a good father is supposed to look like. I don't know how to show affection or be approachable. I want to connect with my wife and kids; I want to listen to them and build their self-esteem and lead them spiritually. But it seems that every time I try, I either freeze up or mess up.

"Although my father and mother lived together for sixteen years of my life, I never really knew my father. He never put his arm around my mother or said that he loved us. He rarely talked to me, and he *never* listened. He didn't hug me at all. In fact, the

47

only time he touched me was when he whipped me. Who can I watch so I don't end up doing to my family what my dad did to me?"

Ted is asking for a mentor!

Sally is strikingly attractive, always gregarious and outgoing, but she doesn't seem to have any close friends. Her kids always look bright and neat—but a bit stiff. Once behind closed doors, her secrets begin to tumble out.

■

"Where do I go to learn a different way?"

■

"I don't know what to do. I love my kids, but I'm scared—what I am doing to my children looks a lot like child abuse. Usually, I am a good mother. But when I'm under pressure and the kids drive me up the wall, I revert and do to them what Mom did to me."

Sally wants a mentor, too.

Jim is two years into his second pulpit ministry. The first one didn't last three years. He is gifted, charming, and definitely not lazy. But something isn't working for him. He calls an old preacher he knew from college days.

"In my heart I want to be a different kind of preacher, a tender servant. My people deserve something better than what I am giving them. But the pastors I saw growing up looked like flashy, cocky, dogmatic manipulators. Where do I go to learn a different way?"

Jim needs mentoring.

Sue and Jerry are thirty-something and realize that if their church is to have a future, people like them will have to shoulder more of the responsibility. Besides, they feel God's tug on their hearts. However, they see problems.

"We would love to become genuine, spiritual leaders—but the only leaders we know seem like distant dictators who only occasionally emerge from their 'smoke-filled rooms' with sour looks on their faces to hand down another edict or scolding for the congregation."

Will Sue and Jerry find a mentor?

Mentoring Defined

Mentor, in one sense, is another dimension of *shepherd,* but with a different emphasis. Shepherds feed, protect, and care for sheep; mentors pull up alongside human beings and model behavior, values, and faith through the shared life. While the shepherd motif is the "big" model for spiritual leadership in Scripture, mentor is nonetheless essential.

Cultural anthropologists tell us that almost every society has had "elders" of some kind. Whether they be tribal chieftains, village headmen, clan leaders, or family patriarchs—most every social unit across history and around the globe has clearly recognized adult role models or "wisdom figures." These "elders" are generally older, more experienced, stronger members of the group to whom the younger look for identity. However, this role is conspicuously absent from modern American culture, at least in formal social structures. Nevertheless, informally—even subconsciously—we long for mentors. We seem to do better when they are in our lives. And when we don't find *positive* mentors, by default, *negative* ones usually find us!

Erik Erickson, well-know pioneer in the field of developmental psychology, is often credited with first tagging these role models as mentors. Of course, Erickson and the rest of us borrow this term from ancient Greek mythology. The story has it that Odysseus, when setting out for Troy, entrusted his house and the education of his son, Telemachus, to a character named Mentor.

Hence, our dictionary defines mentor as "advisor; a wise and trusted counselor or teacher."[1]

Thus, in both the Latin and Greek languages, the term *mentor* literally came to mean "advisor" or "wise man." In later literary and philosophical circles, the term also implied one who broke new ground or who set new trends such as, "Moore and Kierkegaard have become mentors of two different philosophic movements."[2] In today's broad, popular use, the term *mentor* usually refers to a more personal, hands-on role model.

During the early 1990s, poet Robert Bligh—guru of a new men's movement and author of *Iron John*—underscored Erickson when he asserted, "A boy cannot become a man without the help of another man. It may even be a man who is dead. But most ideally a father, grandfather, uncle, or someone to whom he apprentices."[3] Of course, it goes without saying that, while past mentoring research has focused on young *males,* we are very much aware that mentors are every bit as important to young *females* as well.

In spite of its absence in the past few decades, the role of mentor is beginning to find new life in today's western cultures. We understand, for example, that a young lawyer usually emulates an older lawyer, and many physicians are in medicine because of some doctor in their circle of significant others. In a similar fashion, young and new Christians—even those of us who have been at it a while—usually long to be like some admired Christian leader. Mentoring involves all of life—for individuals and for communities.

We naturally tend to become like important figures in our lives—even when we would rather not. Human nature works that way. When our lives are peopled with inadequate, confused, conflicted—but "significant-other"—figures, we tend to inherit their warped ways. In the 1980s, too many young business would-be's aped Ivan Boesky and Donald Trump. In the '90s, some modeled

Madonna, Michael Irvin, or Dennis Rodman. Similarly, warped, toxic religion is sometimes passed from one generation to another through intense, but misguided, religiosity.

But the reverse is also true. When we are fortunate enough to be surrounded by healthy, functional, caring people, we tend to become like them. Loving, nurturing moms and dads pass on healthy family dynamics to their children. Caring, involved teachers inspire students to imitate their style and vision. And godly, spiritual leaders provide healthy role models for growing Christians.

Abraham Lincoln found a healthy role model in Mentor Graham, who influenced Lincoln more than any other single person. Lincoln actually lived with Graham in New Salem, Illinois, for a six-month period. Sometimes they would sit together in the hayfield while Graham taught Lincoln or Lincoln recited to Graham. No wonder that all his life Lincoln spoke with great respect of "my old teacher." One time, because Graham recommended a specific book to Lincoln, he walked six miles to borrow it, then six miles home. The book was *Kirkham's Grammar,* one of the dullest books in the English language, but it shaped Lincoln's prose style and even influenced the Gettysburg Address. By getting Lincoln interested in learning, by teaching him to think clearly and speak simply, Graham started Lincoln toward greatness. Such is the life-molding power of a mentor.

> ■
>
> We naturally tend to become like important figures in our lives.
>
> ■

Erickson held that the mentoring phenomenon is written into the psychological makeup of human beings and that mentors are essential to healthy human development—especially from the

age of four to six. I agree with Erickson. But I take the concept
one step further: I believe that *God* has written the mentor concept into human nature and that is why the concept is written
into the Bible.

Spiritual Mentoring in Scripture

Admittedly, Mentor's name does not appear in the Bible, but
he does!

Jesus mentored his twelve, but his leadership style stood con-
ventional leadership on its head. Jesus drew a bold contrast
between aggressive, competitive, controlling, *worldly* leadership
and *spiritual* leadership.

> You know that the rulers of the Gentiles lord it over them,
> and their high officials exercise authority over them. Not
> so with you. Instead, whoever wants to become great
> among you must be your servant, and whoever wants to be
> first must be your slave—just as the Son of Man did not
> come to be served, but to serve, and to give his life as a
> ransom for many.[4]

Jesus made it clear that his leadership style is based on submission and service, not on authority. Of those pagan leaders who
assert their authority, Jesus said, "Do not be like them." He himself led by serving, and he tells us that where he leads out, we are
to follow."[5]

Paul, too, spelled out mentoring as his leadership model.
"Follow my example, as I follow the example of Christ."[6] "Whatever you have learned or received or heard from me, or seen in
me—put it into practice."[7] To the churches in Thessalonica, Paul
said, *"Live according to the teaching* you received from us," and
"follow our *example."*[8] Paul said his aim was "to make ourselves a

model for you to follow."[9] Paul and Jesus *modeled* their teaching. What they taught was transmitted by *example.* That is, their teaching was what they *did* as much as what they *said.* Example! Teaching! Model! These are all facets of mentoring the faith from one generation to the next and of developing fully devoted followers of Jesus. Jesus mentored, and the apostles mentored.

The mentoring thread runs past the apostles, however. Peter boldly charged spiritual leaders to be *"examples* to the flock."[10] And Paul explained to the elders at Ephesus, "You know *how I lived* the whole time I was with you."[11] "In everything I did, I *showed* you that by this kind of hard work we must help the weak."[12] In so many words, Paul is telling the elders, "I showed you, now you show them."

God expects all of us to mentor others to some degree. At any point in our lives, all of us are being an example to some and following the example of others. But God has given a special responsibility to the recognized spiritual leaders of the church. In Acts 20, when Paul gathered the Ephesus "elders"[13] to give them some final instructions, he said: "Keep watch over yourselves and all the flock of which the Holy Spirit has made you overseers."[14] The Greek word for "elders" in verse 17 is *presbuteros.* This word specifically refers to "the older one." The very term "elder" in the New Testament implies age and experience—not only older in years, but older in the faith.

The elder, the mentor, the *presbuteros,* is a person who has experienced more than others—he has covered more trail. No

> God has written the mentor concept into human nature, and that is why the concept is written into the Bible.

matter where we are on the journey, we are likely to follow the path of other people who have been following Jesus ahead of us. They have passed this way before and will have encountered most anything we are now dealing with. They not only show the way; they give us the heart to go on.

Spiritual Mentoring in the Contemporary Church

Leaders of the church are charged to "encourage the timid [and] help the weak"[15] and to serve and care for the flock.[16] And while it may not be possible for the shepherds to personally, intentionally, hands-on mentor each sheep who needs mentoring, they, along with other church leaders, are to help these needy sheep find godly mentors. To provide for the mentoring needs of their local community of faith, the leaders must be intentional, continually expanding the circle of mentors by equipping others to mentor (we'll talk more about equipping in future chapters).[17]

Plenty of modern-day shepherds are powerful mentors— whether or not they have ever heard the term *mentor*. Cullen and Martha are great examples. Cullen heads a large para-church child-care agency. On Wednesday nights, Cullen and Martha's house is full of people. Those people are his flock—at least a part of it. Some are very committed and focused players in the church. Others are wounded and disillusioned Christians who have no regular church home for the moment. Some are nonbelieving seekers. Cullen and Martha love them, walk through the Bible with them, counsel them, and pray with and for them. In just a couple of hours a week, lives are being changed, and mutually supportive and accountable relationships are being shaped. People who feel disenfranchised are given a place to belong. And some are coming to Christ for the first time. Strong, lasting, spiritually nourishing bonds are being formed between shepherd and flock. Cullen and Martha are mentoring people in Christ.

Interestingly, Cullen and Martha were themselves mentored into this role. They took their cue from Don and Carol—who have been doing something like this in their home for years. An odd collection of the wounded, the faithful, and the seekers gathers in Don and Carol's den. They study the Word and share burdens and struggles. Sometimes someone accepts Christ and is baptized in Don's swimming pool. Oh, and perhaps I should mention—Carol is a busy teacher and Don is CEO of an international corporation. But they are also life-shaping, hands-on mentors—shepherds who smell like sheep.

Hugh is another modern-day mentor—and he was doing hands-on mentoring without even realizing it. A young man, Steve had become a Christian through the life testimony and verbal witness of Kevin. Then Kevin moved away—but Steve was God-hungry. He wanted the skills to feed himself spiritually and to lead his wife Mary to Jesus. We sent Steve to Hugh. For several months, Hugh, although a very busy real estate executive, met weekly with Steve—in what some call a "spiritual power lunch" setting—and mentored Steve to the level where Steve now mentors others. Besides Bible study, Hugh also steered Steve toward taped messages, Promise Keepers, and a small group. Hugh never called what he was doing "mentoring."

> No matter where we are on the journey, we are likely to follow the path of other people who have been following Jesus ahead of us.

But it was. Now Steve is mentoring another brother into Christian family leadership, and as I write these words, Steve has begun mentoring his own lunch-hour flock!

■

In just a couple of hours a week, lives are being changed.

■

The modern-day church shouts the need for godly men and women to serve as spiritual mentors. Spiritual mentors model more than style and vision—spiritual mentors model faith formation, Christ-like lifestyle, ministry skills . . . and so much more. If we don't provide the flock with positive mentors, many sheep will flock to negative mentors by default.

Read on to learn how to be a *positive* mentor.

■

People prefer to
follow those who help
them, not those who
intimidate them.

C. Gene Wilkes

How to Mentor

One young visitor remarked after a couple of encounters with Jake, "So Jake has been pretty visible in your church for a long time? Here every time the doors are opened? A deacon! Well, if Jake is an example of what Jesus does to people, you can color me Buddhist."

No doubt, every good "church-goin' Christian" has met his or her version of Jake. Oh, yes, age and experience do not necessarily make one spiritually attractive. Just because Jake has been over more trail than I have does not necessarily make him a compelling mentor.

A friend of mine describes Jake, one of the older deacons in his church, as "the grand marshall of the foyer and the first line of defense against visitors." Even though Jake's body had logged a lot of miles on his "religion odometer," he wasn't exactly a spiritual luxury limo delivering passengers to the feet of Jesus! What we *are* teaches far more than what we *say*, and this truth can work to bless the church, as well as to harm. In this chapter, we'll take a look at how to be a positive, spiritual mentor.

Winsome Mentors Attract Followers

Winsome mentors are the kind of people who make you *want* to be like them. "Winsome," according to Webster, means "generally pleasing and engaging."[1] Surely, most of us know people like this. Several winsome mentors have blessed me mightily. One was the man who baptized me—J. C. Bailey, who at the time of this writing is ninety-five years of age and still burning with internal fire. Even in recent decades, this man of rugged constitution and iron will could work men half his age into the ground. After forty years of evangelism and church planting in Canada, Bailey, then over sixty years of age, launched into a new chapter of ministry as a missionary to India—where he has led thousands of people to Christ and planted hundreds of churches. In the last few years, this unusual man has been honored for his mission work by several universities, Christian colleges, and Bible training schools.

Not only is J. C. Bailey a great man of faith, with a great passion for evangelism, he is also a colorful character, with a magnetic personality that lights up every room he walks into. When J. C. is in fine fettle, full flight, and rare form, he is one of the most powerful preachers and storytellers I have ever heard—and I've heard a lot.

I wanted to be like J. C. from the first time I ever saw him. A striking trait that punctuates Bailey's impressive visage is the pair of heavy, bushy brows riding above his piercing eyes. The brows dance and twist with every shift of expression and nearly mesmerized me as a child. I remember often sneaking a peek in the mirror to see if my eyebrows were getting heavy enough so I could preach like Bailey!

Later, other preachers fueled my heart for ministry. Just two of these are Charles Coil and Wesley Jones. Charles Coil was a man of absolute integrity, fiery evangelism, and deep compassion. He was also one of the most convicting preachers and compelling storytellers I have ever known. He mentored me in the early days of my preaching as a friend and as the minister of the church that supported Carolyn and me in mission work for eleven years. Later, he founded International Bible College. He went to be with the Lord three years ago.

> ■
>
> Winsome mentors are the kind of people who make you *want* to be like them.
>
> ■

Wesley Jones planted a church in Canada, and his influence as an evangelist was widely felt there. He later served as a missionary and church planter in Indonesia and then in Russia. He took special interest in me when I was a young church planter. Wesley even made the long trip across Canada in 1967, from Ontario to British Columbia, to encourage and mentor me and to speak in a massive evangelistic crusade we launched. We stayed in close touch across some two decades and attended the World Congress on Evangelism together in 1989. Even now, when we communicate, we simply pick up where we left off—though months or years may have passed.

Wesley has battled cancer recently but is still up to his armpits in everyday ministry, with the same sparkle and verve as always. In 1966, he and his wife Beverly were honored at the

Pepperdine University Bible lectures for their outstanding work in ministry.

Although very different men in temperament and personality, both Jones and Coil exuded a common gentle fire and warm affection, with pleasant personality and deep character. I wanted to be like them, and I tried to imitate everything they said and did. I visited often in their homes, and observed their every word and action. I very consciously attempted to treat my wife and my children in the attentive, gentle ways they treated theirs. In the early years, I told and retold their stories and mimicked their mannerisms. In fact, although they first and most pivotally touched my life some thirty-five years ago, I still tell Charles Coil stories and sometimes find myself carrying my Bible like he carried his or borrowing a Jones mannerism or expression. Who would I be had God not sent these winsome mentors my way?

■

He mentored me—and thousands of others— although he died seven years before I was born.

■

Not all of our mentors live during our lifetimes. T. B. Larimore has influenced me more that "any man I never knew." As a teenager, I heard J. C. Bailey tell Larimore stories. While still in high school, I began reading Larimore biographies and then, later, volumes of his letters and sermons. Larimore's flights into enchanting and flawless oratory fired my imagination and drew me to him. His reverence before a transcendent God and his emphasis on big theological themes rather than debates on small issues set him apart from many preachers of his time. Larimore refused to "take sides" in the division threatening his fellowship at the turn of the century. He chose rather to "walk between" and to love all the brethren to both left and right. He simply wanted to bring people to the foot of the Cross, into the footsteps of Jesus, and to the worship and adoration of a majestic and holy God. In my own heart of hearts, I have always wanted to emulate that. Larimore also balanced a love for the local church with a fellowship-wide vision and a passion for evangelism; he stirred my heart to walk the same preaching pathways. Oh, yes, "Brother Larimore" left his mark on me. He mentored me—and thousands of others—although he died seven years before I was born. What a winsome mentor.

Strong Mentors Show Us How to Live

Teaching children songs about Jesus gives me immense joy. All of us—like children—learn best from "show and tell." Of course, this includes an old classic, "The Wise Man Built His House upon a Rock." Since this song is designed for hand signals, it is nowhere near complete without them. Imagine how few children would sing and do the hand signals if I merely explained verbally what they were to do.

"Okay kids! When I say 'wise man,' you point the index finger of your right hand toward a spot one-half inch above your right temple, keeping your elbow bent, with your forearm at a forty-five degree angle to your body. And when I say 'built his house,' place both hands in front of you, four inches from your chest, palms turned toward each other, your fingers pointing up with the fingertips of your left hand touching the fingertips of you right hand, and the heels of your hands separated, representing a roof. And when I say 'upon a rock,' you place the clenched fist of your right hand in the upturned palm of your left hand. And when I say . . . etc. etc."

Do you suppose any of the children would do this? I doubt many would follow these abstract instructions. And even if there should be one little ankle-biter with an off-the-chart IQ who understood exactly what I said, she probably wouldn't try it for fear she might mess up.

So what do I do? Rather than showering the children with explanatory words, I *do* the hand signals as I *say* the phrases, *showing* them how to do it. I show and tell. And they follow. Why? First, because when I show—and not just tell—they *understand* what I mean. And, second, they gain *confidence* that they can do it because they saw me do it first. This is what strong mentors do! They show us how to live.

Many young parents feel a compelling need for Christian parenting mentors. Bert and Sarah are two lovely Christians whose testimony is refreshing, but both of them grew up in acutely dysfunctional families—Bert himself being a recovering alcoholic and adult child of an alcoholic. Bert and Sarah say that one of the richest treasures they have found in the church is a model of healthy Christian families. Bert and Sarah explained, "We never saw how a Christian family, or even a normal family, functions. And now as we rear our children, we need spiritual family mentors."

In today's world, marked by chaotic and broken families, more and more people will need intentional mentoring by older adults in the extended family of the church if they are to learn healthy ways of doing family.

I have watched some tender young couples become like Leroy and Jean. Leroy is an elder, a shepherd of a church. But he is also the CEO of a microchip manufacturing company, serving Fortune 500 computer firms. Business takes him out of town at least one night a week—often even to Asia or Europe. The church Leroy shepherds is mostly young, professional, and upwardly mobile—a fast-lane flock. Like Leroy, his flock has only thin slices of what the world calls "discretionary time." But for a year or more, each Thursday night, a dozen or so young couples ate dinner at Jean and Leroy's house, then together they watched filmed sessions on marriage enrichment and parenting skills, followed by discussion and counsel—mentoring by Leroy and Jean, whose family is long since grown and gone from home. Time investment: 2–3 hours a week; impact: eternal. Leroy and Jean smell like those sheep. And those sheep know the voice of their shepherds, have been fed by their hands both physically, emotionally, and spiritually, and were led in good directions—a fast-lane flock being mentored by cyber-world shepherds.

■

Time investment: 2–3 hours a week; impact: eternal.

■

Today's church not only needs models in family but in many other areas of life as well. We need strong leaders to show us how to handle alcohol, money, sex, stress, temptation, and burnout. We need mentors to show us how to share our faith, how to deal with anger, how to show compassion, how to live with disappointment and grief, and how to do a spectrum of Christian services.

Ray demonstrated servant leadership at its finest one Wednesday evening at an all-church dinner. Hundreds were lined up eager to get their piping hot gourmet plates, when a little preschooler unceremoniously upchucked his whole tummy-full onto the carpet beside the tables. The poor kid was terribly embarrassed. The onlookers sort of froze in their positions. But Ray, one of the respected ministers of the church, made two magnificent servant gestures: First, he put his arm around the little child and wiped the boy's white face with a damp napkin. Then, Ray slipped out of his suit coat, knelt down, and began cleaning

up the pool of vomit. As if on cue, all the "frozen" figures help-
fully swung into damage control of one form or another. This was
fine mentoring.

I personally could fill several chapters describing how others
have mentored me across the years. Here are just two examples.

One church where I ministered had nearly two dozen elders.
Of course, this group included a variety of personality types, but
each was uniquely gifted and qualified to
shepherd. However, as is often the case
among today's church leaders, several of our

■

We need
strong leaders
to show us
how to
handle
alcohol,
money, sex,
stress,
temptation,
and burnout.

■

finest and sharpest men also worked jobs
that kept them out of town much of the
time. Bob was one of these. I love and
respect Bob as much as any man I know.
We have double-teamed many a thorny
ministry situation. But Bob and I are wired
up as differently as is possible in two human
beings. Bob is one of the most left-brain
men I know, while I am off-the-charts
right-brain. I have trouble keeping up with
my keys. Bob is so organized he considers
that a major character defect. I accuse him
of being a boring bean counter who thinks
in rigid columns. He is cerebral, analytical.
I am intuitive, relational. I like stories. He
likes facts. Need I say more? But, we are
alike in one way: we both tend toward
being "control freaks."

Well, Bob traveled a lot and missed
many elders' meetings. While he was gone, the other elders and
staff would carry on without him—working on projects, doing
research, running legwork, and finally laying plans. Then, when

Bob returned from his trips, he would occasionally blow into an elders' meeting, and, by my perception, want to rewrite the whole script, scrap all the work, and change everyone's mind. I grew more and more irritated.

So one day—like a "wise, gentle pastor of the people"—I charged into Bob's office, shaking with frustration. I stood over his desk and berated him for the way he dragged down the morale of the elders and how he torpedoed things good people had slaved on for weeks, etc. With each point my pitch rose and my pace accelerated— and I punctuated my accusations with a stiff index finger. Bob listened a few minutes, then calmly picked up his pen and began jotting notes on a legal pad.

"What are you doing?" I demanded.

"Well, you're talking pretty fast and saying a lot of important things. I need to write them down."

"And what are you going to do with your notes?" I asked suspiciously.

"I just . . . need to think about them," he calmly responded.

By this time, I had begun to settle down and feel sort of cheap. Before too long, I warmed up a little and even began smiling. I think I went so far as to attempt a couple of feeble football jokes. But here is the amazing part: the next week Bob took all of my input, along with input he had gathered from several others, and compiled a multi-paged questionnaire covering the various areas of his performance in tasks and relationships. He told no one about our conversation. He simply distributed his questionnaire to a circle of people who interface with him and asked them

■

Like a "wise, gentle pastor of the people"— I charged into Bob's office, shaking with frustration.

■

to rate him. When he got the results back, would you believe, he made some definite and obvious changes!

My, did I learn something. I couldn't forget what he did. In fact, a few months later, I asked Bob for a two-hour lunch on my nickel, explaining, "This time, I'll bring the pen and pad, and you do the talking. I really want you to help me evaluate my ministry and my relationships."

For over two hours, Bob talked and I wrote. The resulting pages stayed on the corner of my desk for many months. I read and reread them. The man significantly changed my life by his attitude and actions. He was a mentor who showed me how to live. Bob and I have since shared this experience as we co-taught in an area-wide conference on elder/preacher relationships, and I have publicly described this pivotal exchange scores of times.

This is a clear example of what I call mentoring. Bob modeled the Christ-life for me. And he did not do it from a distance—but up close and personal—letting me see that he took me seriously. He showed me how to react to criticism, how to absorb hostility, and how to be a listener. He modeled the need for accountability and feedback. Thank you, good shepherd Bob. Thank you, Lord Jesus, for putting this mentor in my life. I feel deeply imprinted by his hands. I will never take his voice lightly. I love him.

Another occasion when I benefited from mentoring was when the whole church was in major trauma over "Jerod." Jerod was one of those people who was the life of every party. He was bright, funny, good looking, and a former athletic standout. He was highly successful in business, and in the earlier stages of his life, had been deeply committed to Christ and was developing as a spiritual leader. In fact, he was made a deacon in our church and served effectively on visible projects.

But Jerod made a lot of money—fast. And with increasing wealth and independence, he was gradually overwhelmed by the jet-set lifestyle of the nouveau riche during the booming 1970s. His lifestyle progressed from bad to worse—parties, Vegas, alcohol, women, a mistress, and eventually divorce.

Months of prayer and shepherding went for naught.

With the mind-set of powerful people who see themselves above the law and make their own rules, Jerod turned his back on Jesus, turned a deaf ear on wise counsel, and went his own way—yet strangely, he still seemed to want good standing in the church. Because of the far-reaching implications of Jerod's eroding effect on the body of Christ, the shepherds finally, reluctantly, and brokenheartedly applied serious church discipline. After the elders followed the procedures taught by Jesus in Matthew 18, it was time to apply the principles from 1 Corinthians 5 and to express disapproval publicly. But by this time, the church was choosing sides over what should be done.

> He showed me how to react to criticism, how to absorb hostility, and how to be a listener.

Well, I was out of town the day my shepherds made their public statement and so was another of the shepherds. Upon my return, I heard totally contradicting descriptions of what the leadership had done. From some sources I heard, "Sure glad they finally disfellowshipped Jerod." And from others I heard, "Sure glad the elders didn't disfellowship Jerod."

Now the perverse side of me saw an opportunity to make a point to some of the elders (translation: "get in a cheap shot"). I had recently been called to account for verbal carelessness in the pulpit, because I had said some things in a way that left me open to misunderstanding. Of course, *I* thought I had been responsibly careful with my words, and I was defensive of my communication skills. So, now, I chided these good men, "I am supposed to talk to two thousand people twice every week for thirty minutes, making my own decisions about what to say, never leaving room for misunderstanding, and always communicating with total clarity. No foul-ups tolerated. How is it, then, that fifteen of you guys get your heads together, with weeks of forethought, and your combined judgment produces a statement so fuzzy that half of the congregation understands it one way and half the other?" (Yes, I do cringe when I recall saying this. How ridiculous of me.)

Understandably, the room fell dead silent. After a while, one of the elders asked quietly, respectfully, "Well, Lynn, do you have any suggestions on how we might have worded this?" To which I blustered that I did not, but that I was only reminding them to judge me less harshly on my communication skills in the light of their "inept job." Nothing more was said—then.

A few days later, Foy, one of the wisest, most loving of my shepherds, who had sat quietly in that meeting while I had sounded off so unceremoniously, eased up to me and said quietly, "Lynn, I am actually the one who worded the statement we made to the church about Jerod. And I was doing my best to follow the wishes of the group, who felt that we should somehow state disapproval, while making the statement about disciplinary action as vague as possible in order to defuse the polarization!"

Wow! I couldn't believe the thoughtfulness, gentleness, and restraint on the part of these, my shepherds. They had endured my verbal attack, as I spoke so foolishly and critically. Yet they had raised not even a whisper of self-defense—not even an attempt to explain their intentions to me—until the time was right. Now, in retrospect, although I am embarrassed over my behavior (I try to tell myself, "Oh well, that was years ago"), I treasure my warm memory of good shepherds who mentored me by their lives.

Faithful Mentors Inspire Hope

Not only do *attractive* mentors draw followers and *strong* mentors show us how to live, but *faithful* mentors give us hope to keep on trying when we are tempted to give up. Remember the children's song about the wise men? If I will show them how to sing and do the hand signals at the same time, then they will have the courage to do something that sounds hard to do; and they believe it may be possible for them to do it because they saw me do it first! That's hope!

Hope is a big theme in Scripture. Take note of two major examples:

> Therefore we do not lose heart. Though outwardly we are wasting away, yet inwardly we are being renewed day by day. . . . We know that if the earthly tent we live in is destroyed, we have a building from God, an eternal house in heaven. . . . Therefore we are always confident and know that as long as we are at home in the body we are away from the Lord.[2]

> We know that the whole creation has been groaning as in the pains of childbirth right up to the present time. Not only so, but we ourselves, who have the firstfruits of the Spirit, groan inwardly as we wait eagerly for our adoption as sons, the redemption of our bodies. For in this hope we were saved. But hope that is seen is no hope at all. Who hopes for what he already has? But if we hope for what we do not yet have, we wait for it patiently.[3]

None of us can go on without hope. And at certain times, we all desperately need special portions of it. I do. Sometimes I have felt that, surely, if any one in the world has the right to throw in the towel, I do! Have you ever felt like that?

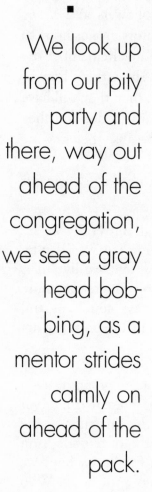

We look up from our pity party and there, way out ahead of the congregation, we see a gray head bobbing, as a mentor strides calmly on ahead of the pack.

Maybe you've felt that nobody else has had to go through what you are going through—you've got pressures at work and stress at home. You've been hurt by friends, hurt by the church, undermined by a trusted coworker, or betrayed by respected leaders. Perhaps disillusionment has set in—disillusionment with church, with yourself—even disillusionment with God!

You may feel that your temptations are just too powerful to overcome, so you think, "What's the use?" Perhaps you are stuck in an intimidating, spirit-numbing, secular environment most of your waking hours, with virtually zero spiritual input. "I, alone, Lord, am the only person in the world who has ever been here and felt like this. I have a right to throw in the towel. Surely anyone else in my shoes would."

I think we all feel this way at times. But then something distracts us from our sad, little, self-absorbed soliloquy! We look up from our pity party, and there, way out ahead of the congregation, we see a gray head bobbing as a mentor strides calmly on ahead of the pack. Then we realize, with full force, that this dear person has seen everything we have and more—in fact a lot we haven't even heard of yet—but he is still moving on. Not only is he still going on, but even though he has been through it all, he has allowed his experiences to make him better instead of worse. He may have been through it personally, or he may have been through it vicariously while ministering to someone else's hurt; but he's been through it. And he didn't give up—he is still pointing you to Jesus.

Even though he has managed many a conflict—he walks ever more at peace. He feels the pain of many people's problems, but he has not grown calloused. In fact, he touches his world with more tenderness and compassion than ever.

He has thrown his arm across a long line of shoulders convulsed with sobs, wiped tears from many a sad eye, and has often pillowed his head at night with his own heart broken—still his face grows continually brighter with joy.

Even though he has heard it all, he listens more intently and cares more deeply than at any time in his life. Although this mentor has been used, burned, hurt, and betrayed—he is not cynical or disillusioned, but smiles—even more broadly on horizons that glow with increasing hope. He is a mentor who gives us the heart to go on.

Flawed Mentors and a Flawless Messiah

As inspirational and encouraging as mentors are, their inevitable imperfections must be acknowledged and accepted. Can you remember when you learned the truth about Santa Claus and faced your first Christmas with those boring mitts and socks, but no toys? "Without toys," you wondered, "what is Christmas for?" And you not only lost some of your innocence, but some of the joy of childhood with it. Maturing a mentor relationship beyond the disappointment of discovery recycles similar emotions.

Dad was my main mentor. My heart *nearly* broke in two when I first noticed some of the clay in my dad's feet. My heart *did* break when my own children began to see the truth of me! When wise men don't know all the answers, we feel some of this loss, too. And when sheep realize that their shepherds aren't perfect, the awareness can be painful.

■

Good spiritual leaders are shepherds, not saviors, leaders not lords, guides not gods.

■

In spite of, and because of, human imperfections, the best mentors know how to point others to Jesus—the only flawless mentor. He was "tempted in every way, just as we are—yet was without sin."[4] Good spiritual leaders know full well that they are only *shepherds,* not *saviors;* they know they are *leaders,* but not *lords;* they understand that they may be skillful *guides,* but they are not *gods.* Christians today need mentors who point to Jesus. Then maybe they will not throw up their hands and quit, but will hang in until the end, "stedfast, unmovable, always abounding in the work of the Lord."[5]

One of the roles that God has given shepherds is that of mentor—winsome, strong, and faithful. God desires *winsome* mentors who naturally attract followers to them; God needs *strong* mentors who do more than *tell* others how to live, but who *show* them; and God needs *faithful* mentors who inspire others with the courage to continue on.

The role of shepherd is an honorable one. Read on, and learn of one more important shepherding role—that of *equipper.*

Section Three:

Equippers

■

I do; you watch.
I do; you help.
You do; I help.
You do; I watch.
You know!
We do together as
a team.

Rusty Caldwell

CHAPTER

6

"Use 'Em or Lose 'Em"

Ordinarily, Tuesday morning's mail makes my day. I love feedback from the church! But the following note from George spoiled my whole week. George's words exploded off the page:

> They ought to sue this church for false and misleading advertising. Your PR blurbs promise all this good stuff, *"Help, Hope, and Home."* Yes, your worship services seemed warm and upbeat when I visited. Then, I joined. But this church has delivered none of its promises. Maybe the sermons offered a bit of *hope.* But no one gave me any *help.* And I sure never felt at *home!* It would take a safe-cracker to break into your circles. I've been here nine months and still feel like a stranger. Take me off your roll, and don't send me any more of that phony propaganda.
>
> Sincerely, George

Church leaders hear outbursts similar to this one every once in a while. And likely, far more are thought but never spoken out loud. Most disappointed newcomers simply vote with their feet. Too many churches seem to lose people out the back door at least as fast as they come in the front. Why? The problem may not always be cold welcomes or irrelevant programs. Often the real villain is ineffective assimilation—failure to usher new members into the heart of the church and make them feel at home and failure to help them use their gifts. Ineffective assimilation, in turn, can be traced almost directly to *inadequate equipping*—which is the point of this section of our book.

Newcomers are initially attracted to a church by something positive. But beyond those first impressions, not all churches deliver on their promises. Of course, not all disappointed guests leave as angry as George. John and Mary Smith's story may be more common.

The Typical Tale of John and Mary Smith

John and Mary first visited Friendly Countenance Church simply because they were invited by a friend. But the Smiths decided to place membership because something about the church itself attracted them. They were primarily drawn (as most newcomers are) by two things. First, they liked the "look" and "feel" of the Sunday morning services. Worship seemed genuine, well-planned, and spirited. It lifted their spirits, involved them, and sent them away feeling great. The preacher connected with their hearts—and in helpful ways, too. Second, the Smiths were attracted to the promises in the newcomers' packet: loads of "involvement opportunities," "helpful programs," and "warm circles of love." So they joined.

Soon, however, John and Mary were no longer visitors being wooed, but members being routinely taken for granted. They were disappointed when they discovered that real life at Friendly Countenance Church bore little resemblance to the helpful picture painted in the newcomers' packet. They had trouble finding their way into the heart of the church. To be sure, many good things were indeed happening in Friendly Countenance Church, but the Smiths couldn't find them. They *did* get assigned a responsibility—printing the bulletin—an important job in its own right. But it felt like boring "busywork" to John and Mary because they were "people persons," and the printing job was totally unsuited to their gifts and outside their interests. They sensed, of course, that something didn't fit, but no one helped them spot the ministries that *did* fit their interests. What they really wanted to do was welcome visitors and follow up on newcomers. But they didn't know where to learn the basic skills required, and no persons were clearly designated to equip them.

John and Mary also saw some circles of fellowship that, on the surface, appeared to be exactly what they needed—but no one invited them in. Why? It wasn't for lack of concern—Friendly Countenance Church was filled with warm and welcoming persons. However, the congregation had developed no user-friendly infrastructure to assimilate people like the Smiths. And no one was trained and assigned to help them.

Eventually, John and Mary felt no hope for meaningful involvement at Friendly Countenance Church, thus no sense of

> John and Mary were no longer visitors being wooed, but members being routinely taken for granted.

ownership and no sense of mission. So, finding themselves unable to connect, John and Mary Smith began to stagnate spiritually.

Ineffective equipping and ineffective assimilation are two of the most critical growth-stoppers in many churches today.

Because the Smiths were not quitters, they hung on for a while, but with dwindling interest. Eventually, without raising any vocal complaint, they quietly left Friendly Countenance Church and moved on to Helpful Circle Church. Since John and Mary made no loud exit noises, the leaders of Friendly Countenance Church did not even miss them until the next computer printout directory was published.

What happened? As in many similar cases, lack of love and commitment on John and Mary's part was not the problem, nor lack of love and commitment on the part of Friendly Countenance Church. Rather, as is frequently the case, the problem was simply that there were no people designated as *equippers* and no infrastructure that encouraged *assimilation*. Thus, they were never brought into a meaningful connection with Christ, his body, or his ministry at Friendly Countenance Church. *Ineffective equipping* and *ineffective assimilation* are two of the most critical growth-stoppers in many churches today.

The Recurring Scenario

This scenario is played out in churches all across the country. People simply find themselves unable to connect. At best, newcomers are often assigned "busywork" or jobs unsuited to their gifts, so they feel like square pegs in round holes. Thus, many leave, often with no vocal complaint. The ones who hang on seldom grow spiritually or commit to useful ministry for Christ. Consequently, church morale dwindles and growth eventually declines.

The same sequence is played out time and again:

✓ People are attracted to churches.

✓ They are initially welcomed and wooed.

✓ They find no place to use their gifts.

✓ Authentic relationships don't happen.

✓ They are soon taken for granted.

✓ Their spiritual growth stagnates.

✓ They leave.

Remember: this decline can usually be traced to ineffective (or nonexistent) assimilation—which in turn comes back to ineffective equippers, or more specifically, to church leaders who miss their calling as equippers.

Healthy Churches Equip Each Member for Ministry

God wants his church to grow. But long-term growth calls for assimilation and equipping skills! Churches that grow help their people find places to serve and help them get the needed skills. Underscore it: Healthy churches develop *leadership styles* and an *organizational infrastructure* that effectively support equipping.

More specifically, the healthiest churches:

• Help incoming members find *genuine relationships*

• Develop effective ways to help each member *find his or her gift*

- Find *specific ministries* in which the members can exercise their gifts

- Equip each member with the *knowledge* and *skills* necessary to accomplish those ministries

- Guide members to become meaningful parts in accomplishing the mission of the church

- Foster *ownership* of the vision and mission of the congregation

This may seem like an overwhelming task, but wait . . . Christ has given churches "gifts" to enable them to fulfill their responsibility to equip members. You can read about these gifts in Ephesians 4:

> To each one of us grace has been given as Christ apportioned it. . . . It was he who gave some to be apostles, some to be prophets, some to be evangelists, and some to be pastors and teachers.[1]

Church leaders are Christ's "gift" to the church.

Even though we no longer have any of the twelve apostles with us today, we certainly have every other kind of leader mentioned here. In Paul's day, *prophets* did more than foretell future events. Actually, their larger role was to speak forth the convicting truth. A prophet is not so much a "fore-teller" as he is a "forth-teller." We have "forth-telling" prophets among us today.

And Jesus gave the church *evangelists*. Not every Christian has the gift of evangelism, but all Christians share the role of witness. And all Christians, regardless of their individual gifts, have their God-given places in the overall evangelistic enterprise of the church.

Then there are *pastors* (shepherds) *and teachers*. Many students of the New Testament believe the phrase "pastors and teachers" in verse 11 does not delineate two different types of leaders, but one kind of leader with two different functions. A better English rendering may be a hyphenated "pastor-teachers." These leaders "shepherd by teaching" or, conversely, "teach by shepherding."

In Ephesians 4, Paul declares that all of these leaders share one specific responsibility: they are to "to *prepare God's people* for works of service" (NIV) or "equip the saints for the work of ministry"(RSV).[2] Don't miss the pivotal significance of the instruction to "prepare" or "equip." While some leaders are beginning to grasp the concepts of "feeding" and "leading" as shepherds and mentors, few appear to have a handle on this critical "equipping" role. In fact, until very recent times, most seemed unaware of the crucial and strategic significance of equipping.

And what are these leaders to "equip the saints" to do? Again, the text is clear: *"works of service"* (NIV), or *"ministry"* (RSV). Equipping includes both the *knowledge* and the *skills* needed to do the works of service or ministry. At least two factors prevent many should-be equippers from passing on their skills. First, many churches, including those of my fellowship, tend to emphasize *Bible knowledge* to the neglect of the actual *skills* required to do ministry. Teaching tends to focus on "what to believe" rather than on "how to serve." Second, anyone who's ever served in a leadership role knows the frustration that frequently sets in when trying to delegate a task or train someone else to do something: we often end up thinking, "This is too hard! It's easier to just do

> ■
>
> Rather than equipping Christians to do the tasks for which God has gifted them, many leaders just "do it themselves."
>
> ■

it myself." Either way, church leaders often end up doing the bulk of the service in the church, rather than equipping the rest of the Christians to do the tasks for which God has specifically given them gifts and opportunities.[3] This factor contributes significantly to leadership burnout. It is also why John and Mary Smith left Friendly Countenance Church and why hundreds have left your congregation and mine!

The Purpose of Equipping Is Growth!

All of Paul's "equipping" talk moves toward a specific goal. The leaders are to equip the saints, so that the saints, in turn, can do the ministry. Why, Paul? To what end? *"So that the body of Christ may be built up."*[4]

Yes! God wants his church to grow! Paul is emphatic. The New Testament makes it clear that God wants the church to be growing in at least three directions:

- God wants his church to grow *numerically*, as lost people are led to Jesus.[5]

- God wants his church to grow *spiritually*, so that each member will no longer be an "infant" who is "tossed back and forth by the waves,"[6] but that each will attain "the whole measure of the fullness of Christ."[7]

- God wants his church to grow *organically*, as relationships become stronger and more mutually supportive and the whole body is "joined and held together by every supporting ligament."[8]

This is God's desire; and when God's leadership style and infrastructure are functioning effectively, healthy, balanced, biblical growth will result. As Paul puts it: effectively equipping Christians will build up the church *because,* then, "each part does its work" (NIV) or "each part is working properly" (RSV).[9]

The specific work of each part is determined primarily by the specific spiritual gift God has given to that part (person). We all have the same spirit, and we all have gifts. But we do not all have the *same* gift.[10] And God has given these gifts for the "common good"[11] or "to serve."[12]

Matching Ministries to Gifts

Equipping requires attention to God's distribution of spiritual giftedness. It does not mean simply dumping jobs onto available bodies. Part of the equipper's work is to help men and women discover and develop their own spiritual giftedness. This means leaders must (1) delegate meaningful tasks to others, who (2) have spiritual gifts and passions suited to those tasks, then (3) equip them with skills to do those ministry tasks.

Many gifted but inactive Christians ride the pews of nearly every congregation—just waiting to be challenged. They will not feel challenged, however, by busy-work assignments that give the superficial appearance of "involvement." But they can and will become and remain excited if they are involved in the congregation's ministry dream and given opportunities to exercise their own unique giftedness—and to be difference makers.

Equipping does not mean simply dumping jobs onto available bodies.

Just think what this could mean for you, weary leaders. As the members of your congregation feel a sense of ownership of the church's mission and as they experience a sense of meaning and significance in their own efforts, a good deal of the stress will be taken off your shoulders. Some works of ministry can be spread around to others, who may indeed be far more suitably gifted than you are for many of the tasks you are now attempting.

Just as a major role for parents is to empower their children to discover, develop, and use their unique giftedness; even so, a major role of church leaders is to help each Christian discover, develop (be trained), and use his or her spiritual gifts in the building up of the body—as "each part does its work."[13]

And the Gift Goes On and On and . . .

> And the things you have heard me say in the presence of many witnesses *entrust* to reliable men who will also be *qualified to teach others.*[14]

Shepherd, what have you received? Whatever it is, God gave it to you so that you might "entrust [that] to reliable people," who in turn, will "be qualified to pass it on to others." To apply this more specifically: Leaders, you are to pass skills and knowledge along and, in so doing, expand the ministry capacity of the church. Leaders, you are meant to equip others (plural) with the equipment you have received, so that they will be able to equip still others.

Hugh and George understand what it means to pass their gifts on to others. At six-thirty, every Friday morning, you'll find Hugh and George at breakfast with an odd assortment of men— some young, some old, some religiously traditional, others push-the-envelope progressive, some core church people, some fringe.

Hugh and George are passionately and tenderly committed to equipping these sheep that have become part of their flock. So each Friday morning they fellowship over breakfast (rotating kitchen chores); then they read from the Word, interspersing their readings with lots of group counseling, mentoring, and equipping; next, they spend time sharing struggles and needs and thanksgivings; and finally, they end their session with a season of earnest prayer. Hugh and George have done this every Friday morning for nearly eight years. And it gets stronger as it goes. Two busy men have found a way to pass on their knowledge and skills to others. These shepherd-equippers smell like sheep.

And so the gift goes on and on and on—like the Energizer Bunny! And the ministry capacity of the church expands, indefinitely . . . till Jesus comes!

Good equippers do it
like Jesus did it: recruit
twelve, graduate
eleven, and focus on
three.

Lynn Anderson

How the Chief Shepherd Equipped His Flock

Troy is a good friend. He is open-minded and always on the learning edge. But it takes him a while to think things through, and he wants all the details he can get. I wasn't surprised when, several sessions into a "shepherding conference," he motioned me to join him on the front steps, established strong eye contact, and wanted more answers. "Okay. I'm convinced. Elders are to be equippers. But *how* is this done?"

I wasn't merely trying to be cute when I answered, "Troy, do it like Jesus did it!"

Actually, a youth minister first taught this concept to me.

Some time back, David Lewis, a youth minister I worked with for two decades, taught me, the rest of the staff, and the elders something he discovered by "necessary accident." This was

David's first youth ministry, but he and his wife, Pam, obviously had received enormous gifts for it. They connected with kids on a grand scale. They threw themselves as fully as possible into the life of each teenager—they attended ball games, sat through hours of one-on-one, and had kids into their home. So, in the early stages, while the youth group was small enough for David and Pam to keep up with, the youth ministry flourished. But before long, the numbers mushroomed so that even with their enormous gifts and energy, working longer hours and moving faster, there was no way David and Pam could keep up. In fact, the ministry began to put strains on their family and to wear on their physical and emotional health.

Eventually, David and Pam recognized their limits and wisely backed off to ponder their dilemma. At a mountain cabin, they mulled through the question, "How would Jesus deal with our situation?" Gradually it dawned on them that Jesus *did* deal with their situation—or one very much like it.

Jesus, though fully God, was also fully human with the physical, social, and emotional limitations that go along with being human. And rather than spreading himself so thin that his relationships drifted to the shallows and his own health eroded, Jesus calmly, systematically devised an effective game plan: He would equip others to accomplish the ministry. He structured the number and intimacy of his relationships into manageable configurations.

Jesus' Style of Equipping

David and Pam noticed that Jesus' ministry touched people on several different levels of relational intimacy.

At the first level, Jesus fed and preached to *thousands.*[1] We read in Luke 12:1, "When a crowd of many thousands had gathered, so that they were trampling on one another, Jesus began to speak." We might call this Jesus' "mass media ministry." At this level, he touched many, but with limited intimacy. Most equipper/shepherds will likely find themselves, at times, teaching large crowds—especially those shepherds who are good public speakers. So far, so good. But not yet good enough for the best equipping.

Second, Jesus worked with *hundreds*—for example, the circle of one hundred twenty loyal followers who gathered in Jerusalem in Acts 1:15. His relationship here was somewhat more direct than with huge crowds, but still not deeply intimate. Again, in today's church, some excellent shepherding can take place in similar settings—for example, when leaders address the whole church, or a large segment of it, to challenge the flock on budget goals, vision, strategies, objectives, or the like.

The third circle of Jesus' relationships narrowed sharply as he sent out only *seventy-two* for a special mission.[2] Church leaders today often work with their "groups of seventy," so to speak—perhaps they delegate a project to a large Bible class or commission a team to run VBS.

> Gradually it dawned on them that Jesus *did* deal with their situation—or one very much like it.

But equipping moved front and center in Jesus' ministry at the fourth level, when Jesus zeroed in on only *twelve* men. A very different dynamic existed at this level than at the larger levels. This intimate circle of twelve became his near constant companions for three years. Mark says succinctly, but significantly, that they were "with him."[3] It was while they walked those roads together that Jesus equipped them in the context of intimate shepherd/mentor relationships.

Of course, to expect today's church leaders to cut loose and travel full time for three years with the handful of people they are equipping would be unrealistic. But today's church leaders *can* adopt Jesus' relational and highly *intentional* style of equipping.

David Lewis decided to follow Jesus and be *intentional.* When David and Pam returned from their reflective retreat, they immediately set about to employ Jesus' strategy in their youth ministry. They prayerfully tapped out a dozen couples and asked them for a specific commitment, making sure the couples clearly understood the expectations. David asked each couple to commit themselves to approximately ten young people for at least one year. This commitment included having these young people in their homes every Wednesday night to eat with them, study the Bible with them, pray with them, and build authentic relationships with them. David called these groups "huddles," a name that later caught on across the continent in some youth-ministry circles. He challenged each couple, should they accept, to develop fully devoted teenage disciples who would in turn be equipped to win and nurture others. That was the goal. They also asked the couples to pray for several days before they gave their answer.

And my, did that strategy work! In the next few years, scores of teens came to Christ and to maturity in Christ. Not only did the ministry flourish, David and Pam's sanity—and their ministry—were preserved. And best of all, the ministry expanded, as many others were "equipped for ministry."

Something else happened. Out of this experience, a pivotal ministry style emerged, which, across some twenty-five years, has become the model for spiritual leadership in the great Highland Church in Abilene, Texas. In fact, some of those original "huddle leaders" are now elders in that church. In addition, this "huddle" system of youth ministry, which spread to hundreds of congregations, is still alive and well today.

On a fifth level, *Jesus had a few especially close friends.* Jesus didn't share the same level of intimacy with all twelve of his disciples. Like all normal human beings, Jesus had special friends—Peter, James, and John appear to have shared a special closeness with Jesus. We see this, for instance, at the Mount of Transfiguration.[4] Just these three were with him. Again, in the Garden of Gethsemane, Peter, James, and John stayed nearer to Jesus while he prayed than the other nine.[5] And after Jesus ascended to heaven, these three occupied visible roles in the early life of the church.

> ■
> Not even Jesus was capable of an unlimited number of intimate relationships.
> ■

In other words, the relationships through which Jesus' equipping ministry flowed were *natural human* relationships. Normally, human beings can manage only a limited number of intimate relationships. And Jesus was fully human—wired up as a human being. Not even Jesus was capable of an unlimited number of intimate relationships. Small wonder my friends David and Pam Lewis could not manage over a hundred intimate relationships at once. They were beginning to see that church leaders are equippers. Later they would see that, in some senses, every Christian is meant to equip some other Christian.

Modern church leaders must learn from Jesus and "equip the saints" by following Jesus' example. However, like Jesus, their humanity demands that they limit the number of intimate relationships to a realistic ratio. This means that leaders must learn to be satisfied with decreasing levels of intimacy, as their circles of relationship expand outside the inner circle. They must also empower those they equip to equip still others to equip others.

Are you an equipper? As my shepherd friend Grady Jolly said repeatedly, "Find someone who knows more than you and learn from that person. And find someone who needs what you know and teach that person. Every Christian is a *student;* every Christian is a *teacher.*"

> ■
>
> Leaders must learn to be satisfied with decreasing levels of intimacy, as their circles of relationship expand outside the inner circle.
>
> ■

Now, sixth and finally, let us follow Jesus one level deeper into his relationships to *"one . . .* disciple whom Jesus loved."[6] Of course, Jesus loved all his disciples, but apparently he was especially tight with John. Jesus did not feel it inappropriate for him as a religious leader to pull up beside *one* especially close, personal friend within his "congregation." So, my friends, David and Pam concluded, "If Jesus needed to employ such natural yet varied levels of relationships, surely youth ministers—and elders and deacons and worship leaders and other church leaders—need to do the same thing."

Some churches, however, have been slow to recognize this. For example, a decade ago the employee policy manual of a large church in the southwest required that "Staff ministers of the church shall not form their personal friendships from within the congregation." Presumably, this was a well-intentioned attempt to avoid charges of cliquishness or favoritism by their ministers. But how unlike Jesus. How unnatural. And . . . how terribly damaging. The fact that within a few months of each other, more than one divorce occurred in ministers' families on that staff and another staff spouse suffered emotional collapse is likely more than mere coincidence. Flawed leadership styles not only impaired the health of that church, but nearly destroyed some of its ministers.

By contrast, Jesus' equipping-style leadership helped shift the direction and nurture the health of the Highland Church. Along with David and Pam Lewis' influence, the elders of that church began to sense their need, as leaders of that church, to focus their shepherding and equipping on specific flocks of manageable sizes—from within the larger congregation.

A New View of Shepherding

I recall stepping into the elders' conference room one winter's evening to see one of our "senior" elders, Art Haddox, sitting alone, slumped over in his chair, with his elbows on his knees and his hands covering his face. Tears trickled out between his fingers, enough tears that some had reached his elbow.

"Art, what's wrong?" I asked.

"I feel so overwhelmed," Art responded. "God has called me to be a shepherd of this flock. We have nearly two thousand members here, and try as I might, I don't even *know* but a fraction of them. So how can I shepherd and equip them one-on-one? I am so tired. And I feel as if I'm failing as a shepherd."

That encounter still haunts me all these years later. How many leaders feel overwhelmed and guilt-ridden by unrealistic demands? Or, in congregations where the leaders do not understand their equipping role as shepherds, how many flocks are starving and wandering and finding no place of ministry, for lack of Jesus-style equippers?

The conversation with Art Haddox was underscored by a letter received not long after from Dr. Milton Bessire, tendering his resignation as an elder. A medical doctor, Milton had also been a tireless and tender hands-on shepherd of that same church for many years. He was truly a servant of people and a man of prayer.

■

They were functioning more as a board of directors than as hands-on shepherds, mentors, and equippers who smell like sheep.

■

I shall never forget the shocked silence and the spirit of conviction that settled over the room when Dr. Bessire's resignation letter was read. His reason for resigning? "So that I can be free to do more shepherding!" Bingo! How ironic and tragic and ludicrous. Resign from being a shepherd so that he can do more shepherding? Something is obviously wrong with this picture!

Something else came into clear focus that day. Doctor Bessire obviously had "a flock" within that mega-congregation that he knew by name and who knew his voice—because he shepherded them. Dr. Bessire's resignation and Art Haddox' painful dilemma triggered a season of introspection by that whole group of godly elders. Other leaders besides Milton, Art, and the Lewises began asking themselves: "Am I actually equipping any specific persons? Do I really have a flock? Will I ever have one if I keep operating in this executive style? How do I free myself up to have time for real shepherding, mentoring, and equipping? After all, that is what I signed on for to begin with."

Those elders fell under the conviction that they were distorting the work of spiritual leadership by functioning more as a board of directors than as hands-on shepherds, mentors, and equippers who smell like sheep. They realized they had gotten caught up in marathon meetings, setting policy, administrating, wrangling over budgets, and caring for facilities. They were even bogging down in discussions over the color of drapes and carpets, while some of their drowning sheep were about to go under for the third time. Ironically, this was happening, in spite of the fact that the congregation was blessed with over a hundred deacons, many of whom were at least as well skilled in administration, finances, construction, legal matters, etc., as were any of our elders and could have taken on these responsibilities.

When Dr. Bessire died, although it had been years since he was officially called an elder, he was still shepherding, and he left behind a bereaved flock. However, God had long since used his well-articulated resignation letter as a pivotal motivator in that church.

Dr. Bessire understood that elders are hands-on shepherds, not a board of directors. Art sensed that he could not manage an infinite number of shepherding relationships. David Lewis discovered the small circle, equipping model of Jesus. God combined these and other insights in his blueprint for equipping. Through Milton's letter and Art's tears, time had come for David and Pam Lewis' discovery to impact the leadership style of the Highland elders.

The door opened for the elders of that church to begin thinking of themselves more as shepherds and less as managers. They began to take seriously Jesus' style of equipping and delegating. One by one, most of the shepherds began to focus on his own natural flock within the larger congregation, rather than each of them trying to be the personal shepherd/equipper for all two thousand plus members of that church. These leaders also began to view themselves *less* as "permission/grantors/withholders" and *more* as equippers who equip "lay people" and empower them for ministry. This gradual and healthy trend in the leadership styles at Highland continues till this day.

Dear reader, please note: For leaders to focus on a smaller circle is not the shirking of responsibility—not by a long shot. In fact, in this way, over the long haul, far more people will be equipped and "doing ministry"; consequently, the flock will be better shepherded, more ministry will get done, and the church will "build itself up in love, as each part does its work."[7] Plus—weary leaders will feel their burdens lift.

Jesus' Finished Work

Observe again what happened with Jesus. Jesus said early in his ministry, "My food is to do the will of him who sent me and *to finish his work.*"[8] To "finish the work God had given" was obviously high on Jesus' list of urgent goals. "As long as it is day, we must do the work of him who sent me. Night is coming, when no one can work."[9]

Strikingly, at the end of his ministry, Jesus reported to his Father, "I have brought you glory on earth by *completing the work you gave me to do.*"[10] When Jesus said, "I have completed the work," he could not have meant that his "salvation work" was done. His salvation work was to be done on the Cross. Rather, John 17 must refer to some work he had done on earth between John 9 and 17. Apparently, Jesus meant that he had completed the work of equipping his disciples, because he explains toward the end of his prayer, "As you sent me into the world, I have sent them into the world."[11]

In a sense, Jesus had duplicated himself in his disciples; his leadership style—shepherding, mentoring, and equipping—had become theirs. He was sending *them* into the world, equipped to continue the work for which God had sent *him* into the world; and they did it the way he had done it.

As Acts and the epistles record the apostles' ministry, we see the results of Jesus' equipping. It is no accident that Paul and other apostles followed Jesus' style of equipping in their own ministries by taking "interns" with them wherever they traveled. In fact, Paul not only set this example before his "trainees," he also charged them to so train others who would in turn train still others. Remember, Paul charged Timothy, "The things you have heard me say in the presence of many witnesses *entrust to reliable men* who will also be *qualified to teach others.*"[12]

■

When you equip a fellow believer for ministry, you give God pleasure.

■

Jesus' style of equipping is not too hard to understand, but it can be difficult to implement. It is not complex, but it is costly. Equipping calls for consistent investment of time in another person's life and patience as that person appears, at times, to barely crawl up the learning curve. It also calls for vulnerability and openness—and intentional effort. The rewards, however, are immeasurable: It brings spiritual fulfillment to both the equipper and the equipped; it expands the ministry capacity of your church. Best of all, when you equip a fellow believer for ministry, you give God pleasure.

We teach what we
know, but reproduce
what we are.

John Maxwell

CHAPTER

Equipping through the Shared Life

This chapter puts contemporary wheels on Jesus' equipping model for spiritual leaders, rolling it into the twenty-first century, down your street, and in your front door. The Jesus style of equipping carries clear and monumental implications into the role of modern-day spiritual leaders. Jesus equipped his men through the "shared life." The men he trained, in turn, charged their trainees to do the same thing. So surely, leaders in today's church who are charged with equipping the flock for works of ministry are meant to do their equipping through the "shared life"—Jesus style!

However, let us repeat a word of caution: Some of the material in the next few pages spells out the absolute ideal, describing what Jesus himself was able to do in three years—apparently with no other job and with no family responsibilities—in the lives of twelve men who also apparently had no other commitments. Obviously, most church leaders—who are busy business and professional people with family responsibilities and whose flocks also are mostly busy, professional people with families—cannot be expected to duplicate Jesus' pace. We are not laying out a blueprint that must be followed. Rather, we will pinpoint basic *principles* from Jesus' style of equipping. These principles, while certainly transferable to the twenty-first century, must, of course, be applied in ways that fit today's settings. But these eternal principles do provide a workable paradigm for equipping, and they can move spiritual leaders toward effective use of whatever time frames, group sizes, and situations are realistically available to modern, fast-lane shepherds.

Following are some principles of equipping that can be observed in the ministry of Jesus.

Frequent and Long-Term Contact

First, Jesus had *frequent* and *long-term contact* with those whom he equipped.

Just how often was Jesus with his twelve? Matthew records sixty-seven different occasions when Jesus and his disciples spent quality time together. John tabulates seventy-three. Most of these were extended associations. In fact, as we skim the three years of Jesus' ministry, we find precious little time when Jesus and his disciples were apart.

On our first trip to Palestine, Carolyn and I spent one day enjoying an excursion from Jerusalem to the north end of Galilee. Even though we rode in an air-conditioned Mercedes Benz and drove over paved highway, the round-trip took a long day. But we broke up our day with periodic stops for frosted Cokes and McDavid hamburgers. As we wound up and down, round and round, through the Galilean hills, we couldn't help thinking about how Jesus and his men had made this trip many times. They had traveled over dirt roads and dusty paths—and on foot, not in a comfortable limo! They had no refreshing Cokes at McDavid's in the heat of day and no soft beds at Holiday Inn come nightfall. It dawned on us that, basically, Jesus and his disciples spent most of three years on the road, *walking!* And as they walked and talked, Jesus built his life into these men, equipping them for the ministry that lay ahead.

Again, I am not suggesting that church leaders today quit their jobs, leave their families, and hit the road for three years straight to train twelve men. Unfortunately, however, today's shepherds rarely spend much time at all equipping specific sheep from their flocks.

> ■
>
> Jesus and his disciples spent most of three years on the road, walking!
>
> ■

You tell me: How can shepherds equip saints to do their ministry in one hour a week of formal class time, transmitting mere information to a classroom full of people at different stages and with varying needs? Life-styles and values cannot be imparted through a couple of quick greetings per week in the aisle or foyer, in the midst of a crowd—much less practical skills for personalized ministry.

What then? Is there any hope of transmitting the faith from this generation to the next in the midst of our fast-paced life-styles? Yes, I think so. But, obviously, not without definite intentionality and some major adjustments.

Warm and Loving Relationships

Second, Jesus enjoyed a *warm and loving personal relationship* with his trainees. His role was not one of boss to employees. He was not the CEO, with the Twelve somewhere down his payroll "food chain." Jesus did not reside in the officers' quarters while the Twelve bunked in the barracks. On the contrary, Jesus called them his "friends."[1] He traveled with them, ate with them, even washed their feet. "He now showed them the full extent of his love."[2] He connected so authentically that one disciple (maybe all of them) felt that he was the "disciple whom Jesus loved."[3]

If this is the way our Chief Shepherd related to those whom he was equipping for ministry, how can today's shepherds expect to equip the saints merely through policies hammered out behind thick, oaken boardroom doors, through edicts handed down from on high, or through serving as arbiters in disputes? How can they expect to influence genuine life changes by posing only as answer-men in Bible class or through ecclesiastical policing action when someone runs afoul of their wishes? How can they communicate effectively through bulletin memos alone, without hands-on, eye-ball-to-eyeball contact in a shared life?

Honest Exposure of Emotions

Third, those equipped by Jesus were *exposed to his emotions.* Remember John 11:35, "Jesus wept." This is the shortest verse in the English Bible, yet it carries one of the heaviest messages. And what made Jesus cry? After all the high-blown theories are offered about why Jesus wept, we finally come down to the simple truth: Jesus wept because Jesus cared. When he heard the sobs of the sisters of Lazarus, Jesus simply could not hold back his own tears. I doubt he tried. And the Holy Spirit, along with the New Testament writers, seems proud of that.

While the scene at Lazarus' graveside is strong medicine, for me the cleansing of the temple reveals Jesus' raw emotions even more forcefully.[4] Jesus flashed white-hot anger at the money changers in the temple. No selfish tantrum or pent-up resentment this. Not at all. Rather, this was real righteous indignation. Someone said, "You can measure the character of a man by the size of the things that make him angry." The object of Jesus' huge anger that day was no little thing.

Jesus watched the worshiping pilgrims come and go. No doubt he saw the hopeless looks on many faces—like that on the face of our imaginary friend Ben, for example. Ben had saved for years to make his Jerusalem temple pilgrimage. Life was ordinary in his hometown, and local synagogue meetings were not very exciting—hard benches and dim lights. Old Ezra droned on so when he read the scroll that even godly old Asher sometimes nodded off. There didn't seem to be a lot of transcendence and glory around there. "Sometimes I wonder if I'll ever see God," pondered Ben. "Ah, but next year in Jerusalem! Yes, Jerusalem. That is where the great priests and prophets headquarter. That is where the magnificent temple, the place of God's very presence, stands watch over the city. Surely, when I go up to Jerusalem, I will see God!"

> ■
>
> After all the high-blown theories are offered about why Jesus wept, we finally come down to the simple truth: Jesus wept because Jesus cared.
>
> ■

Imagine Ben reaching the border of Judea. See him dismount and kiss the sacred soil, then jump back on his beast and hurry toward the Holy City. Feel his excitement swell at his first glimpse of Jerusalem; hear his pulse pound inside his skull when the shining dome of the majestic temple finally bursts into view.

Once inside the gates, Ben's trembling hands untie his sacrificial lamb. He had raised that lamb in his backyard and carried it all the long journey—especially for this day. But the examining priest gruffly rejects Ben's lamb. "An old tick bite on the left ear. No matter. We have temple-approved lambs for sale. We'll take yours on trade. The price? Oh yes. I know that's four times what you pay in Bethinia. But this is Jerusalem—at Passover, no less. Law of supply and demand, you know. Oh, I am sorry. Only temple currency, please. That's right, the exchange rate is two of yours for one of mine."

> ■
>
> "You can measure the character of a man by the size of the things that make him angry."
>
> ■

Although the glow of the Holy City is a bit tarnished by now, pilgrim Ben continues to move toward the altar, eager to connect with Almighty Yahweh. Along the way, he struggles through the chaotic din of priests who sound like circus barkers trying to outshout one another, all hawking lambs and doves at exorbitant prices.

Finally, Ben finds himself at the altar, and he stops a moment to reflect. He closes his eyes and tries to let his senses drink in this long-awaited encounter with God. Ben's heart overflows. But his meditation is rudely interrupted. The priest in charge is trying to move at least one sacrifice a minute through his station. God suddenly seems very far away from Ben, farther even than he had seemed in the little synagogue back home. But in spite of a heavy heart and numbed emotions, Ben has no choice but to watch as the priest adroitly and impersonally slaughters his lamb as he hurries Ben along. Profoundly disillusioned, Ben finds himself feeling unclean for even being present. Tears come. Even before the lamb's blood stopped spurting, Ben was hurrying toward the exit gate. On the way out, he ran into the same priest who had taken his "blemished" lamb and saw that he was selling it to another pilgrim at four times the price he had paid Ben.

In mind's eye, I can see Jesus watching as Ben and an endless line of other pilgrims stumble toward the gates to find their donkeys for the long, long road home. Their faces look like blank masks and their vacant eyes like burnt holes in their skulls—chins dropped to chests, all hope drained from their shoulder lines. A hoarse whisper, "I guess it is not meant for me ever to see God."

Jesus' emotions build until he could be still no longer. See him move resolutely toward the first money changer—eyes ablaze, wrist flicking a whip that cracked like a rifle shot. With strong carpenter's arms Jesus heaves over a table, sending money flying, lambs scurrying, and pigeons fluttering. Then on to the next table. Then to another. This area of the temple was large enough that it may have taken him an hour—or two—to do his work. All the while he shouts, "My Father's house was meant to be a house of prayer, and you have made it a den of thieves."

One wonders if the disciples stood slack-jawed, marveling, "Wow! I've never seen him this upset before."

Early in my preaching ministry, one of my mentors warned, "Lynn, don't ever express your emotions in the pulpit. If tears come, people will think you are weak, or if any anger shows, they'll think you lack self-control; and you will lose credibility." That mentor is a good man whom I still respect very much, but that piece of preaching advice had to be some of the worst I have yet received. In the first place, I am not wired up for calm detachment. For me to attempt to give the impression that I am not emotional would be as phony as an undertaker trying to look sad at a fifty-thousand-dollar funeral. I doubt I could pull it off. But far more important, my mentor's advice—while well intentioned—was *exactly the opposite of Jesus' style.*

Shepherds today who follow the Chief Shepherd's style of equipping will be vulnerable and expressive, unafraid to reveal their emotions. They will make the best spiritual leaders.

This is confirmed in the following note I received from a friend.

> One time, I was requested to be at a meeting with two elders, myself, and Charles Coil. I remember thinking at the time that this was a strange combination of persons to be invited to a meeting and wondered what was going on. However, when I got there, one elder began passing around a letter in which he confessed adultery. I will never forget that man staring at the carpet in humiliation and shame. And I will also never forget seeing Charles Coil walk over to the man, get down on his knees, and cry as he hugged him. Something about seeing Charles Coil's heart broken over the sin of this man marked me deeply.

This was an up-close-and-personal look at a good shepherd's emotions.

Coach Wally Bullington, mentioned earlier in this book, is another shepherd who is unashamed of emotions. Once Wally asked me to accompany him on a visit to a dear friend and brother in Jesus who had strayed far from Christian fellowship and was separated from his wife and involved in an affair with another woman. The man had once been in the inner circle of ministry and friendship in the church. I shall never forget Wally down on his knees before this brother, weeping as he begged the dear friend to soften his heart, give up his sin, and come back to relationship with Jesus and God's people. Even now, my eyes moisten and my heart aches with this weeping shepherd. Even though Wally was unaware of it, he was equipping me that day by revealing his emotions.

A Variety of Shared-Life Experiences

Fourth, those equipped by Jesus observed him *in a variety of life settings.* Run your mind across the story line. Find Jesus with his disciples at the synagogue—on the road—by the sea—by a hillside—*on the road*—in the temple—by a well—in a boat—at a wedding—*on the road*—on the mountain—in the garden—in court—at banquets—*on the road . . .*

During their travels with him, the Twelve saw Jesus in nearly every conceivable life setting. As Max Lucado pictures it, "They saw the wax in his ears, the dandruff on his shoulders, heard him snore, smelled his breath, saw him sweat. They were run out of town with him and saw thousands give him the red-carpet treatment."[5]

How will Christians be equipped for ministry today? Likely, not very well if they only see their spiritual leaders in a controlled

> I shall never forget Wally down on his knees before this brother, weeping as he begged the dear friend to soften his heart and give up his sin.

environment at church, when everyone is dressed up, talking religion, and on their best behavior. We've got to get out into "their world."

God stamped this on my heart in bold block letters one afternoon at Rocky Gillette's Texaco station. Rocky Gillette was rough, gruff, and tough. Not exactly the guy I'd want mad at me in a deserted alley. He had done his share of drinking and fighting, but I liked Rocky. We always got on well and came to respect each other.

Most of the gasoline I burned in those years came from Rocky Gillette's Texaco down near the church, so it was easy to get pretty well acquainted with the gang that hung out there. However, I usually filled up en route to or from the office, so few of them ever saw me when I was not dressed in a suit and tie.

One day, my phone rang over at the church, and it was Rocky. Out of the blue and with no preliminaries, Rocky got straight to his point, "Lynn, I think I need baptism."

"How come, Rocky?"

"Well, I saw Jim come down to the front of your church last night, crying and snorting, and I couldn't believe my eyes. Jim is one the roughest guys in the town, and we have never liked each other. In fact, don't tell anyone, but I've always been a bit scared of him. I think he's scared of me, too. But last night I saw you baptize Jim, and half the church came up and hugged him after. Got me thinking. If God could forgive Jim, maybe he could forgive Rocky Gillette. Besides, if that church would accept Jim, maybe they'd accept Rocky Gillette."

In time, Rocky became a genuinely converted Christian, although, frankly, he never was much of a churchman. His ministry, however, was with the gang that hung out at the Texaco. Rocky would hire people who were basically unemployable, for the express purpose of teaching them how to get and hold a job—

which a lot of them did once Rocky got finished with them. While they worked for him, if they messed up, he would coach them on how to do better. Some of these trainees stole from Rocky, but he didn't fire them. He just took them out behind and "worked them over, West Texas style—in the name of Jesus, of course," and told them, "Now, get back to work, and don't do that again—or it'll be worse for you next time. You ain't never gonna hold no job stealin' from your boss."

Well, one evening on my way in from quail hunting, wearing jeans, boots, a hat, and a two-days' beard, I wheeled my pickup into Rocky's. I knew Ellen, the young woman on the pumps, but she didn't see it was me till I handed her my credit card. Then she burst out so loud everyone in the place could hear, "Oh, it's you, Reverend! I'm sorry. I didn't recognize you *with your clothes on!*" Rocky's whole ragamuffin entourage fell out in raucous laughter at my expense.

> ■
>
> "Oh, it's you, Reverend! I didn't recognize you with your clothes on!"
>
> ■

In actual fact, Ellen was telling the truth. From her perspective, up until that afternoon, every time she had seen me, I wasn't wearing "real clothes." I was wearing my "preaching uniform," a suit and tie. She had never really seen me as part of her life-setting—nor had Rocky.

Now, all these years later, it wouldn't surprise me to hear that story retold on that corner. The gang at the station never let me forget that incident. But from that moment on, my relationship with Ellen and all of them moved to a far more authentic level. Hopefully, they also came to see that the followers of Jesus don't all wear stuffed-shirt suits. Beginning with that change of clothes, they saw me in a new life-setting—as a real person. And things went better from then on as I attempted to lead Ellen toward Jesus and further equip Rocky for ministry.

■

The backyard barbecue might be a better equipping place than the Sunday-morning podium.

■

In final preparation for this book, I called Rocky to get his permission to use this story and learned the good news that Ellen (not her real name) recently celebrated her eighth year of sobriety. And Rocky told me that two brothers, whom he had trained, had gone on to become successful business owners with several employees, and now *they* are the trainers.

All church leaders—whether ministers, small group leaders, elders, etc.—who learn equipping from the Chief Shepherd will do well to share a variety of life-settings with those they are charged to equip. Jesus-style equipping might call for some leaders to do some fishing or little league coaching; others might need to go on backpack trips or play volleyball. Seems the backyard barbecue might be a better equipping place than the Sunday-morning podium. Maybe the sheep could learn more from the shepherds if they could see them "with their clothes on," as they deal with temptation, competition, stress, anger, and confusion. Or the shepherds might take the sheep along on hospital visits or to a home where death has just visited or to sit in on an evangelistic Bible study or to watch an equipper lead a small group. Equipper and equippee might follow Jesus' style and walk *together* into a variety of life settings.

A Life of Integrity

Fifth, those equipped by Jesus saw *consistency between his teachings and his actual behavior.* He *practiced* the same life-style that he *taught.* As the Hebrew writer puts it, Jesus was "tempted in every way, just as we are—yet was without sin."[6] Peter also explains that he "suffered, . . . leaving . . . an example, that [we] should follow in his steps. 'He committed no sin, and no deceit was found his mouth.' When they hurled their insults at him, he did not retaliate; when he suffered, he made no threats."[7] Point is, Jesus practiced what he preached. Today's spiritual leaders must as well.

Jesus took it one level up. He usually *demonstrated* his truth first, then *explained* the implications of what he had done. Possibly the clearest example is when Jesus washed the disciples' feet and then explained the implications his actions had for them.

> Jesus . . . got up from the meal, took off his outer clothing, and wrapped a towel around his waist. After that, he poured water into a basin and began to wash his disciples' feet, drying them with the towel that was wrapped around him.[8]

This was Jesus' demonstration. Then came his explanation.

> Do you understand what I have done for you? . . . Now that I, your Lord and Teacher, have washed your feet, you also should wash one another's feet. I have *set you an example* that you should *do as I have done for you.* I tell you the truth, no servant is greater than his master.[9]

Jesus dramatized his message—by doing, then talking.

In this particular case, Jesus set up this drama and initiated the explanation. But more often in the gospels, Jesus explained things in response to questions about something he had done. His words always carried enormous weight because of the magnetic credibility of his deeds.

So also, spiritual leaders in today's church equip out of the credibility of their lives, demonstrating consistency between what they say and what they do. As the old poem puts it: "I'd rather see a sermon than hear one, any day. I'd rather someone walk with me than merely point the way."

> ■
>
> The very attempt to pull off a perfect image demonstrates a lack of integrity.
>
> ■

Discerning leaders, however, know that they will be imperfect in their efforts to "walk the talk." In fact, for most of us, the very attempt to pull off a perfect image would, in itself, demonstrate a lack of integrity. Rather, shepherds of *integrity* will be open regarding their humanity and humbly vulnerable and honest about their struggles and need for grace. Further, healthy leaders will surround themselves with people who will hold them accountable and offer needed support. In so doing, they will model a life-style, which, in spite of the equipper's own failures and frailties, will equip the saints to keep on following Jesus with integrity.

Of course, prudence must be exercised here. I am not suggesting that being open and vulnerable requires leaders to dump their guts indiscriminately. Furthermore, not every naive lamb is ready for a frontal view of his or her shepherd's spiritual nakedness. I am not suggesting mere self-effacement. Self-bashing can undercut credibility, too. Such prattle often merely parades a false humility. I must not perennially bad-mouth one of God's sanctified ones—even if that person happens to be myself. Rather, I am suggesting that leaders stay in touch with and acknowledge their own vulnerability and authentically acknowledge dependency on God. Shepherd and flock must continually, openly, and honestly remind each other that all of us are kept sanctified *only* by the strong embrace of his amazing grace— not by some virtue or strength of our own. The moment I do anything in order to appear better or stronger than I really am—no matter how small it may seem—I have begun a deadly deception, and I set myself up for bigger and more horrendous things to come.

To illustrate this point, one minister friend tells of driving up to church at midnight to pop in and encourage the youth group that was practicing for a Christmas program. The hour was late, and he was in a hurry; so he wheeled up into the fire lane, jumped out of his car, and ran in. No big deal. After all, it was just for a moment, and after all, he was *the minister!* The next day, one of his staff members informed him that a teenager had spotted his car illegally parked and had wondered out loud, "What jerk would block the fire lane outside a room full of young people?"

To my astonishment, the minister later apologized to the whole church for his presumption and recklessness, and he even pointedly invited them to keep holding him accountable. For him, that one fairly innocent act was actually an early warning that he presumed privileged status, that he felt somewhat impervious to wrong doing, and that he had taken the first self-deluding step in a direction that could ultimately be disastrous. By his open confession before the church, he was practicing an honest awareness of his own vulnerability; and in this simple but powerful way, he modeled *integrity.*

Time Balanced Between Problem and Possibility People

Fifth, Jesus *balanced time between problem people and possibility people.* Today's spiritual leaders do well to follow his example and spend at least as much time with possibility people as they spend with problem people. Train the strong, in addition to helping the weak. Some people are in a healthier position to be *allies in* ministry rather than purely *objects of* ministry. Tread carefully here, however. Obviously, life empowered by the love and compassion of Christ dodges no problem people. They caught the eye of Jesus, so they had better get significant portions of our compassion as well. Besides, some problem people have the potential to become possibility people. And yes, all human beings are problem people in the sense that we are all flawed sinners. On the other hand, allowing ourselves to be consumed *only* with problem people drains our energies, and in the long haul, actually narrows the scope of our ministry.

So, in spite of his compassion for problem people, Jesus also invested in the lives of functional people who had enormous leadership potential. Peter, James, and John, for example, led a business before Jesus equipped them for leadership in his church. Luke the physician cared for sick bodies before penning prescriptions for sick souls. Matthew was a public figure before Jesus called him into the mission—not to mention Nicodemas from the Sanhedrin. And Paul was a well-educated rabbi before Jesus made him a global missionary and core theologian for the centuries.

Besides consuming a spiritual leader's time and energy, problem people can give the shepherd a warped and jaded perspective on reality, leading to overwhelming feelings of frustration and hopelessness. For example, in the early days of one church planting in Canada, Carolyn and I found our energies increasingly consumed by very troubled people. A new mission work can attract the unstable fringes of the community first. I shall never forget a weary moment of insight as Carolyn and I were driving home from yet another marathon "emotional first aid" session. We turned to each other and asked simultaneously, "Do we know any sane people?" When I repeated the question, Carolyn answered, "I don't!"

Possibility people lift leaders' spirits and supply positive, hopeful perspectives. More importantly, possibility people generally mature and take on responsibility sooner than problem people. Equipper shepherds can more quickly delegate part of the mission to them. Thus, the burdens of the ministry will be spread and shared more rapidly and the overall ministry capabilities of God's church immeasurably broadened. Thus, in the long run, more people—of both problem and possibility varieties—can be reached and served. In addition, when the spirits of leaders are lifted and their loads lightened, many a weary shepherd can be rescued from burnout that may otherwise cut short his or her usefulness. I believe this is at least one reason that Paul told leaders to be equippers and that Jesus modeled the spreading of leadership burdens through equipping possibility people and delegating responsibility to them. Jesus also gifted each member of his church for his or her place of ministry.

> Some people are in a healthier position to be *allies in* ministry rather than purely *objects of* ministry.

So again, in summary, Jesus equipped his apostles through a shared life. The apostles then employed Jesus' style of equipping with the leaders they trained. The apostles in turn charged those coming after them to continue equipping others. Church leaders are charged to "equip the saints for works of ministry" or to "prepare God's people for works of service."[10] This is God's plan. He was intentional. Surely God wants today's shepherds to follow the equipping style of the Chief Shepherd, his apostles, and their students. Surely God wishes today's church to identify as its leaders those who are already imitating Jesus' style of equipping!

When we work God's delegating and equipping agenda, we will not only take grinding burdens off our own backs, but we will lay the foundations of an expanded and more effective church-wide ministry for the future.

For every elder, minister, small group leader, worship leader, etc., a key question is, "Who are you equipping?"

But a more important question is, "Are *you* following the Chief Shepherd?" In the end, only he can equip us with what we need most. He said, "I have come that they may have life, and have it to the full."[11]

PART TWO

A Biblical Look at Elders:

The Sort of People They Are

Section One:

A Character Sketch

■

Example is not the
main thing in
persuading others;
it's the only thing.

Albert Schweitzer

CHAPTER

9

Just What Is
an Elder?

Part 1 of this book, under the heading, "A Biblical Look at Spiritual Leadership Principles: The Sort of Things Leaders Do," explored three models for spiritual leadership. These models fit all types of spiritual leaders—elders, small group leaders, Sunday school teachers, even parents and those who mentor friends. However, in Scripture, these three models—shepherd, mentor, and equipper—are applied first and foremost to elders of the church. Thus, this second section, titled "A Biblical Look at Elders: The Sort of People They Are," will focus more on who and what elders are—and especially on the *qualities* of elders. However, any man or woman aspiring to be a better spiritual leader of any kind will find help in the practical guidelines presented in the pages to follow.

But before we go any further, I want you to pick up a pencil and get ready to write down some names.

Imagine that you've hit a snag and need a coach. Maybe temptation has taken you under for the third time. You feel broken, in need of mending. You have just done the worst sin of your life—again. Then again. And you don't even know how to confess it, let alone extricate yourself. Who do you call?

Or suppose you face a major decision—marriage, business, career—and you need guidance as you weigh your options. Perhaps a parenting challenge has pushed you beyond desperation or an important relationship isn't working. Maybe your business is going down the tubes or your marriage is in deep trouble. Or perhaps the doctor has just told you that you have a life-threatening illness, or maybe your faith is on the rocks or some other "biggie" has you in mortal straits and sorely in need of safe and wise spiritual counsel.

Where will you turn for help?

Who are you most likely to turn to when your back hits the wall? What specific names come to mind? Jot down the names of the first three people you think of .

Do it now.

Okay. Stop and ponder. Why did you select these particular people?

I have worked this exercise with a lot of people around the country and have kept mental notes on the reasons they give for selecting specific names. Maybe some of their reasons match yours.

> "I know ____, ____, ____ well. I already have some sort of relationship with them."
>
> "I see ____, ____, ____ as experienced and competent enough to give wise counsel."

"____, ____, ____ are available. I can always find them."

"____, ____, ____ are approachable. I find it comfortable to be open with them."

"____, ____, ____ are hospitable, express love to me in several ways, and often create opportunities for conversation."

"I have watched ____, ____, ____ make sound spiritual decisions in their own lives."

"____, ____, ____ know the Word of God."

"____, ____, ____ are respected by the people I most admire."

This little exercise is one of the most *practical* ways I know to define what an elder is. (We'll look at specific biblical qualities in the pages to follow.) An elder is the kind of person you would choose in a crunch: an elder has the experience, character, and vision to guide, comfort, and advise the sheep of his flock.

Christians often long for guidance from a wise and gentle "big brother" or "big sister." God wired us up this way. When we hurt, we long for help and comfort from someone who has been where we are. When life overwhelms us, we look for someone who is strong and experienced. In the midst of confusion, we seek people who can give steerage through treacherous waters. When shaping our lives, we reach out for mentors.

And God has supplied what we need. Most circles of Christian relationships include God's gift of several mature spiritual guides and wise counselors who serve in various leadership roles—official and unofficial. But at the heart of God's leadership gifts to the church is the very special function or role of *elder.*

The biblical concept of elders may be new to some readers, but I think you will find that this God-defined, God-instigated leadership role is as vital to the twenty-first century as it was to the first—and as perfectly suited.

What Is an Elder?

First and foremost, elders are *shepherds*. And what is a shepherd? A shepherd is someone who has a flock. Shepherds in Bible days were not day laborers who showed up for work in the morning at a stranger's pasture, put in eight hours, and then went back home. Rather, shepherds lived with the sheep—day and night, year after year. Shepherds helped birth the lambs. They led their sheep to pasture during the day and protected them at night. The sheep knew their shepherd's touch, recognized his voice, and followed no other shepherd. There was a genuine relationship between the shepherd and the sheep. In fact, through long time and frequent touch, the shepherds *smelled* like sheep.

Just so in today's church: elders are not strangers merely plugged into a job. Rather, elders are people who already have a flock, who already are serving as shepherds. The process of appointing elders is simply the process of acknowledging those who have been shepherding for a long time. It is recognizing those who have attracted flocks through the genuineness of their lives, the consistency of their service, and the authenticity of their relationships. A person officially becomes an elder when through one means or another, his flock says to the rest of the congregation, "You too need this man as your shepherd." And the rest of the congregation says, "Shepherd us also."

Elders are also *mentors*—persons who have walked over the trail ahead of us—a long time in the same direction. They attract us to their ways. They show us how to live. And when we are tempted to give up, they give us the courage to go on because they have kept on, in spite of everything.

Finally, elders are *equippers*. They prepare Christians to do works of service. Through one-on-one time with both problem and possibility people, they help each person find his or her own spiritual gift. And they guide each person into a specific ministry, matching tasks to gifts and passions. Then, equippers train each member with skills needed to do his or her specific ministry.

Above all, whether shepherding, mentoring, or equipping, elders do their best work through *relationships*. Thus, the authority of an elder grows, not out of a title emblazoned across a church letterhead, but out of the quality of the elder's life: the credibility of his walk with God, the genuineness of his service, the authenticity of his relationship with the sheep. This is why the qualities of his life are so crucially important.

■

Elders are not strangers merely plugged into a job. Elders are people who already have a flock.

■

How the Bible Defines Elders

In the Bible, three key words describe the function of elders. We are first introduced to these three terms at an emotion-packed going-away party on the beach near the tiny port of Miletus. On a trip to Jerusalem, Paul the apostle stopped in to say good-bye to his friends. He had an ominous foreboding of his own death; so he told his friends he would never see them again and charged them with their responsibility as leaders of the church:

From Miletus, Paul sent to Ephesus for the *elders* of the church. When they arrived, he said to them: . . . "Keep watch over yourselves and all the flock of which the Holy Spirit has made you *overseers*. Be *shepherds* of the church of God."[1]

■

The authority of an elder grows, not out of a title emblazoned across a church letterhead, but out of the quality of the elder's life.

■

Note carefully the three words used in Acts 20, above. These same three words are also used by Peter (1 Pet. 5:1–4) to describe these special church leaders: "elders" *(presbuteroi)*, "shepherds" *(poimaenoi)*, and "overseers" *(episkopoi)*.

The first of these terms, *presbuteroi* (usually translated "elders") most simply means, "older ones who lead because of experience"—older in years and older in spiritual experience.

The second word is a metaphor, *poimaenoi* (in English, usually "pastors" but more literally "shepherds"). Modern American churches often refer to preachers as "pastors," but the biblical word is "shepherds," and in these contexts is not used for a singular leader, but describes a plurality of leaders within a given congregation—or those most commonly known as elders.

Episkopoi is the third descriptive word. Most English translations say "bishops," although some say "overseers." However, the imagery suggested by these popular renderings is rooted more in seventeenth-century King James images of ecclesiastical hierarchy than in the meaning of this word in New Testament times. A more helpful and accurate translation of *episkopoi* might be something like: "guides," "caretakers," "leaders," or "those who watch on behalf of." In fact, when the word *episkopoi* is used to describe spiritual leaders, the sentences in which it is used (both in Acts and 1 Peter) describe their work in pastoral terminology. As Carl Holladay says,

> The constituency of the *episkopoi* is a "flock" and their task is to "feed" it. Whatever is implied in "overseeing," cannot be divorced from the role of "shepherding." . . . In fact, to whatever degree such terms as "superintendent," "overseer," "guardian," and "bishop" are used to emphasize the rank of the position, to that degree they mitigate the true meaning of the term *episkopoi.*[2]

Or, as H. W. Beyer says, "It is plain that the point of the office was service, and service alone."[3]

what are "Qualities"?

The core criteria for elders are found in 1 Timothy 3 and Titus 1. Take a moment to read these passages:

> If anyone sets his heart on being an overseer, he desires a noble task. Now the overseer must be above reproach, the husband of but one wife, temperate, self-controlled, respectable, hospitable, able to teach, not given to drunkenness, not violent but gentle, not quarrelsome, not a lover of money. He must manage his own family well and see that his children obey him with proper respect. (If anyone does not know how to manage his own family, how can he take care of God's church?) He must not be a recent convert, or he may become conceited and fall under the same judgment as the devil. He must also have

a good reputation with outsiders, so that he will not fall into disgrace and into the devil's trap.[4]

An elder must be blameless, the husband of but one wife, a man whose children believe and are not open to the charge of being wild and disobedient. Since an overseer is entrusted with God's work, he must be blameless—not overbearing, not quick-tempered, not given to drunkenness, not violent, not pursuing dishonest gain. Rather he must be hospitable, one who loves what is good, who is self-controlled, upright, holy and disciplined. He must hold firmly to the trustworthy message as it has been taught, so that he can encourage others by sound doctrine and refute those who oppose it.[5]

These two passages of Scripture have traditionally been referred to as the "qualifications" of elders. I prefer the term "qualities" rather than "qualifications." This is not merely semantics. On the surface, the word "qualifications" sounds unfriendly. It conjures up images of "specifications"—like "specs" for auto parts or calibrated instruments. But on a more significant level, "qualifications" are often reduced to some sort of "checklist," which is rather mechanically applied. Also, this checklist perspective tacitly implies that every elder must fully meet every requirement on the list in order to make the cut. This perspective also tends to ignore other important qualities not mentioned on these lists.

Paul would likely be shocked to see his material used as a checklist. Rather, in these letters to his ministry interns, Paul simply employed a literary device common to his times. The ancient Greeks frequently used general character sketches, arranged in list form, to profile a good person. An often cited example of this literary device in ancient secular literature is Diogenes Laertius' sketch of the stoic's concept of a good man: "He must be married;

he must be without pride; he must be temperate; and he must combine prudence of mind with excellence of outward behavior."[6]

Odosander, another Greek of antiquity, broadstrokes the character of the ideal commander. "He must be prudent, self-controlled, sober, frugal, enduring in toil, intelligent, without love of money, neither young nor old, if possible the father of a family, able to speak competently, and of good reputation."[7]

> Paul would likely be shocked to see his material used as a checklist.

The style used to describe these ideal persons in secular literature bears striking similarity to Paul's style in the pastoral epistles. When Paul used this literary form, he did not intend to provide a complete and absolute list of qualifications. He simply broadstroked two character sketches. The one in Titus pictures the sort of men who would make good shepherds among God's flock of Christ-followers on the island of Crete, and the other in 1 Timothy sketches the sort of men who would make good shepherds in the city of Ephesus. That explains, at least in part, why the two sketches differ: the two widely different settings required different leadership traits and qualities.

"Fitting" Elders

Shepherds do not come "one size fits all." "Elder" is not a generic category of person who can transfer his leadership directly from this congregation to that. A good elder in one church may not begin to make a good elder in another. The Holy Spirit, through Paul the apostle, zip-coded his character sketches to specific churches. Apparently, God intended that each shepherd should *fit his church situation.*

Course, ribald, rural Crete was not at all like refined, ordered, urban Ephesus. The issues faced by the one church were not the same as those faced by the other. The two cities obviously called for somewhat different qualities in their elders—thus the differences in Paul's leadership sketches. Notice, for example, that for Crete an elder must "hold firmly to the trustworthy message as it has been taught, so that he can encourage others by sound doctrine and refute those who oppose it."[8] The next verse explains why. Because, Paul says, "there are many rebellious people, mere talkers and deceivers," who are causing trouble and "must be silenced."[9] Significantly, the congregational needs at Ephesus did not require these specific qualities given for Crete. Thus, he did not mention them in his letter to Timothy.

Of course the *general* needs of one congregation will be similar to another—basic human nature being the same the world over. So most of the qualities named for Ephesus match those named for Crete. But each congregation was in a unique setting, with its own personality and its own cast of characters creating its own problems; thus to some degree, each church had its own *specific* leadership needs.

Today, as well, no two churches are exactly alike. Each faces its own challenges. Appropriately, then, in addition to the leadership qualities sketched in Scripture, a local congregation might compile its own list of qualities important for shepherds in its particular setting. Actually, most congregations do this either consciously or unconsciously, written or unwritten.

For example, one congregation I served had a long-standing policy requiring that their elders be nonsmokers and teetotalers. Of course, there is no book, chapter, and verse for either of those qualities. But years ago that church sensed that *in their church and community* most people simply would not respect the spiritual leadership of a man who smoked or drank. Another church in a different setting may see no need to require these qualifications, yet it was certainly appropriate for that church to require them.

My friend Dr. Carroll Osborne, whose roots run to rural Arkansas, says (not entirely facetiously, I think) that "an elder in the Black River bottoms of Arkansas would not likely command much respect unless he owned high-class coon dogs. If a man didn't have enough sense to know good dogs, how could he possibly have enough sense to lead a church?"

■

> A good elder in one church may not begin to make a good elder in another.

■

My father attained only a sixth-grade education and spent very little of his time in the city—even less around business leaders. He understood virtually nothing of the complexities posed by urban racism, classism, sexism, pluralism, or runaway materialism. Yet he served for years, unusually effectively, as a shepherd of a small church in western Canada. Dad, in turn, was mentored by Russell Elford, a rural man, who in his whole lifetime, never once lived in a city or even a small town. Dad and "Brother Elford"—both whom I consider spiritual giants and very suited as spiritual leaders in their native settings—would hardly be equipped to shepherd a heterogeneous urban church of college-educated professionals, entrepreneurs, and CEOs like my current church family in the Park Cities of Dallas. This takes shepherds with a new set of skills.

Raising the Bar

The work of elders is exceedinly challenging. It was in the first century. It is now. Obviously, shepherding, mentoring, and equipping, defined by the three words used in Acts 20 and 1 Peter 5, along with the character sketches in 1 Timothy and Titus, add up to some mighty lofty expectations. Perhaps the following excerpt from Max Lucado's booklet on biblical leadership will put things in perspective:

> I can remember as a youngster having a high jump bar in the backyard. I spent many hours throwing myself over the bar, which was a cane fishing pole, and landing in the pit, which was an old mattress. I was proud of my achievements until the day my big brother and his friends came by.
>
> They raised the bar. When they jumped, their minimum was my maximum. They began where I finished. They jumped higher than I'd ever dreamed. When they left, the bar was at a new level. And I had a new concept of what it meant to jump high. They had set a new standard.
>
> Elders are called to raise the bar in the church. They set the example and lift the standard of what it means to be a Christian. Ideally, an elder should do for your life what my brother's friends did for my high-jumping. Being with them should cause us to think higher thoughts and set higher dreams. The life of an elder should inspire us to raise the bar in our home life, prayer life, character, and dedication.[10]

The pastoral epistles definitely set high standards for elders. But in so doing, Paul not only elevates the ideals of leaders, he also clarifies the vision of followers and helps us, as sheep, size up shepherds. Good sheep can sniff out good shepherds: they are the men who are *already* shepherding and have *tended a flock* long before they were thought of as "elder candidates." If you want to be "good elder material," get out and live among the sheep. Spend so much time with them that you actually *smell* like them.

My friend Jim found a man who smelled like sheep. Jim was returning to the Lord from wild singleness, when he began dating a girl from a Christian college, who pointed him back to church—and to a shepherd.

"In fact," Jim explains, "I actually met this girl at a church in Dallas where I had begun worshiping on my way back to the Lord. We fought, fussed, and argued all the time. We argued in front of people—even at church. One Sunday, our song leader invited me to dinner at his house. He was a very gentle, kind, and gracious man. Although I did not know him well, I admired him greatly. After dinner he brought up my dating relationship and gently talked with me about how a Christian man treats a Christian young lady. I felt this man gently shepherd me that evening. I was not surprised when some months later the congregation asked him to serve as an elder."

Oh yes. Even wayward lambs can spot good shepherds. But Paul's letters to Timothy and Titus make it easier.

Shepherd, mentor, equipper—three models that add up to strong, spiritual leaders. *Elder, shepherd, overseer*—three words that give dimension to the role of the biblical elder. These concepts help us see what elders *do.* Now we turn to 1 Timothy and Titus to see what kind of persons they need to *be.*

The remainder of this section will not attempt to specifically and exhaustively examine each of the "elder qualities" in 1 Timothy and Titus. Rather, we will look at these character sketches under some broader headings: elders are to be men of *experience,* men of *character,* and men of *vision.*

■

It is only as we
develop others that
we permanently
succeed.

Harvey S. Firestone

10

Men of Experience

Okay. I admit it. Inexperienced elders make me nervous. Give me an elder who knows his way around the track. Some readers may attribute this preference to my own "advancing years," but I felt this way when I was thirty-five. And long experience confirms my feelings—so does the Bible. From reading the two spiritual leadership character sketches in 1 Timothy and Titus, it is obvious that elders must be *men of experience*.

Experience with Life

Men Who Have Been *Around* a Long While

First, as we've already stated, the word "elder" means "older." Elders are men who have *been around* a good long while. More technically, the very word *presbuteroi* (elders) implies age, maturity, and experience. Current North American culture, to its profound loss, places little value and respect on age. But the Word of God stands in judgment over this shallow view. And most cultures—of the world past and present—place a high premium on the wisdom and insight that come only through long experience. Time lends perspective. Experience deepens one's wisdom and refines his or her judgment. Long years of living present ample opportunity to check out blind alleys. There are things in an older person's heart that a young person just cannot know.

■

"I am not going to trust my soul to someone who has not yet been through midlife crisis!"

■

My friend and former colleague, David Wray, an excellent minister who has also been an elder for some years (which means he has managed many crises in human relationships), puts it this way, "I am not going to trust my soul to someone who has not yet been through midlife crisis!" No book, chapter, and verse in the Bible can be found for that insight, but it will ring true to our most experienced readers.

An elder must be someone who has *lived long enough to have logged a track record.* This record answers some critical questions: Does he know himself? Does he know people? Can he stand pressure and remain calm in the midst of confusion and conflict? Has he dealt gently with people, even those who hit him with bitter criticism and harsh confrontation? Has he nurtured successful relationships? Across the years, has he demonstrated the validity and usefulness of the principles by which he claims to live his life? Have his years left a trail of people made better because he passed their way? Oh yes, an elder must be "elder"—someone who has lived a good long while. Time has been his training ground; it has also become a *measuring stick*.

Men Who Have Been around *Jesus* a Long While

Second, an elder must be *a man of long spiritual experience*—one who has been *around Jesus* for a long time—not merely a person who has blown out an acre of birthday candles. Paul warns that an elder should not be "a novice" or "new convert."[1] Some people run hot and cold. Three years in the church, three years out, three years in. . . . Some years ago I met Hal (not his name), who for years had waffled in and out of the church. When I first met Hal, he had been "in" for over two years and was in a "super spiritual" phase. During this "in" cycle, he was appointed an elder. Tragically, however, before a year had passed, his life came unraveled again. Those who appointed him had not watched his walk in the Lord long enough to know whether Hal was spiritually stable enough to lead the church. The apostle Paul warned: "Do not be hasty in the laying on of hands."[2] Had Paul's advice been heeded, Hal's church could have avoided tragedy. The potential elder must be viewed through these questions: "Has he been a Christian long enough that we can trust him to stay straight? Can we let our weight down securely on his commitment?" Good elders must have walked with the Lord for a long time!

Men Who Have Been around the *Devil* a Long While

A good elder has not only been around the Lord a long time, he has been around the devil, too. He has wrestled with sin and temptation—and won. Long years of spiritual combat toughen and season a person's spirit. Churches are best led by men who are veterans of the battle. These men have learned enough about sin—up close and by experience—to be wise to Satan's ways. And they have hammered out practical methods to deal with the evil one.

Such a person can offer wise advice, flowing out of spiritual maturity. When I take my needs and struggles to this shepherd, he will not only be "shock proof," but he will be able to listen with his heart and genuinely understand me. He will offer me something more than platitudes, and he will point me to the resources that have helped him.

Experience with the Word

An elder must also be a person who has been *around the Bible* for a good long while, a man who is thoroughly *experienced in the Word*. Scripture clearly describes a good shepherd as "able to teach";[3] he is called "pastor and teacher."[4] Teaching is inherent in the very role of "eldering."

Our grandson Connor was three years old and secure in his world—part of which was a church day-care center where his mother worked part time in one room while Connor "went to school" in another room. One afternoon, the teacher settled the kids in for their story time and then explained, "Today we are going to talk about Jesus." Whereupon, Connor stood up, thrust his hands onto his hips authoritatively and confronted his teacher, "Well. If you're gonna talk about Jesus, you need to have a Bible in your hands." Connor may have deserved a D for deportment, but he should get an A for accuracy. His point was right on target. The church needs men who have long-time experience with the Word of God, whose passion for the Scripture stretches far beyond scholarly interest and burns with light for the Way. The church needs elders who *"live* in the Word," not merely *"study* the

Bible." Our best passions can be stirred by a shepherd who lives under the Cross with blood in his tracks and a Bible in his hands.

The man who is experienced with the Word has assimilated the Bible into his life, so that his teaching serves up life resources and strength to others. This teacher will not only be at home with the *Bible,* but at home *sharing* it with his flock. He is one who stands regularly in the midst of people with his open Bible in his hand. He understands their needs and feelings and is able to connect the Scriptures with real-life issues.

A teaching elder opens himself to his flock. As he teaches, we can sense whether or not he is approachable or wise. We get a feel for his understanding of human nature. We peer into his heart. If his teaching is on target, we trust his leadership. Then, when the storms hit, we are most likely to gravitate toward a teaching elder as our sheltering fold. This is God's design. Oh, how the church needs *teaching* elders.

However, I must add a word of qualification: "able to teach" does not necessarily require that the shepherd be skilled in public speaking nor that he be a public personality. Many excellent teachers of the Word flounder in front of a large class, but set souls on fire when across the table from one or two people with an open Bible. While he may not be a Bible scholar or gifted with words, because he is at home with *the* Word, he imparts more than Bible knowledge alone. He shares real-life resources and strength.

> ■
>
> Our best passions are stirred by a shepherd who lives under the Cross with blood in his tracks and a Bible in his hands.
>
> ■

With that in mind, however, beware lest the one-on-one idea become a neat cop-out for persons *called* elders, but who actually don't teach in *any* setting. The important question is not, "Can he teach a class?" The real question is, "Does he teach?"

Paul also says a good elder "must hold firmly to the trustworthy message"[5] for two reasons: one positive, one negative.

Men Who Teach the Word *Positively*

Hopefully, the bulk of a shepherd's teaching will be of the *positive* kind—serving up positive spiritual nourishment for his flock. Elders are charged to "encourage others by sound doctrine."[6] Doctrine, however, is not merely information. It is not merely ethereal concepts such as justification, sanctification, redemption, predestination, and all those other words that end in *-tion.*

Rather, doctrine, from Paul's pen, is practical teaching about how to live day to day in the trenches. For example, Paul tells Titus, "Teach . . . sound doctrine," and then he spells out what he means: "Teach the older women . . . [to] train the younger women to love their husbands and children. . . . Encourage the young men to be self-controlled."[7]

In other words, good elders are meant to encourage and instruct real, live people in healthy patterns of daily Christian living. Of course, we receive encouragement when someone we love and respect effectively teaches us abstract biblical information. That kind of teaching is surely necessary for us to think "Christianly." However, the lights really come on when that trusted teacher connects Scripture to daily life and spells out real-time practical help. We should be able to look at an elder and answer the question, "Whose daily life do I see growing and flourishing under this man's teaching?"

Men Who Teach the Word *Negatively*—When Necessary

At least part of an elder's teaching, on the other hand, must be negative. Scripture says that in addition to encouraging people by "sound doctrine," an elder will also be able to "refute those who oppose it."[8] A leader cannot effectively "refute" those who "oppose sound doctrine" unless he is strong enough in the Word to detect false doctrine. But refuting those who oppose sound doctrine is more than defending what we've always believed. Indeed, what we've always believed is not necessarily sound, and what is new to us is not necessarily unsound! An elder cannot know with confidence what is "sound" if he relies too heavily on a hired expert for his answers. He must know the Word *himself*—and know it thoroughly enough to confidently and clearly identify the difference between truth and error.

The best teachers of Scripture will not merely cite proof texts, they will hold a larger view and firmer grasp of the Bible so that they can perceive the implications of the sound and unsound uses of Scripture. When you or I bring a major spiritual problem to a man of God, we do not so much need a proof text as we need a principle; not so much a reference as a resource; not so much a verse of doctrine as a vision of deity. We want someone who can walk us through the Word, show us the face and heart of Jesus, and then zip-code the Word to our specific needs.

> ■
>
> An elder cannot know with confidence what is "sound" if he relies too heavily on a hired expert for his answers.
>
> ■

In summary, then, an elder must be a man of the Word: a man who knows it, lives it, and can teach it in ways that excite the faith and shape the lives of others. Good shepherds bless the flock with insights into God's heart and practical skills for living Christ-honoring lives.

Experience with Successful Family Relationships

Life experience and Bible-teaching skills alone, however, do not necessarily make an effective spiritual leader. Life experience and Bible knowledge must be tested in the *crucible of family relationships.* When Paul mentions family relationships in his lists of qualities, in effect he is asking, "Is this man's faith actually 'working' in the most intimate and intense of relationships?" And his relationship management skills are most convincingly demonstrated within his family. Here is where a leader's *true* character comes through.

If a man's life cannot stand the scrutiny of his wife and children, we dare not put our souls under his care. If he is not able to maintain healthy relationships at home, why would the church want his advice—much less his spiritual leadership? Thus, in both 1 Timothy and Titus, Paul underscores qualities demonstrated in the success of family relationships.

Success in His Relationship with His Wife

At the top of the list: "What about a leader's relationship with his wife?" Paul said an elder is to be the "husband of but one wife."[9] Literally, in Greek, this means a "one-woman man." At least four key insights tumble out of this phrase.

First, this line obviously addresses *moral purity.* An elder cannot be one who chases women or even has "eyes full of adultery."[10] Few factors shatter trust as deeply as sexual sin. His commitment to sexual purity—even his emotional marital fidelity—must be obvious and without question to his wife and to all who know him.

Second, beyond unquestioned fidelity, "one-woman man" also carries positive implications. It not only describes what he will not do, it tells us what he *will* do. A one-woman man manages and nourishes a *healthy intimate relationship* with his wife. They are happy together. He knows how to communicate openly with his wife. His healthy marriage shows evidence that he will be able to manage and nurture healthy, successful relationships and open communication in a church. Good shepherding definitely depends on such skills. How comfortable we feel around an aging couple who love and respect each other and who obviously enjoy being together. And what a healthy environment such people spread in a church.

> ■
>
> If a man's life cannot stand the scrutiny of his wife and children, we dare not put our souls under his care.
>
> ■

Third, "one-woman man" describes this person as a *lover.* He knows how to love his wife, how to make her feel securely cherished and valued. Why would we expect a man to love God's church when he has not done a good job of loving his own wife? Conversely, how warmed and enriched we feel under the care of a shepherd skilled in the art of love. A man who brings a glow to the face of his wife will brighten the lives of his flock as well.

Fourth, and possibly most important of all, a one-woman man demonstrates by the stability of his marriage that he can *keep covenants.* He is a promise keeper. He will keep his marriage covenant—no matter what—because he is a covenant-keeping man. And he is a covenant-keeping man because he worships and honors a covenant-keeping God.

> ■
>
> At the root of most failed marriages today, we find shattered covenants.
>
> ■

At the root of most failed marriages today, we find more than communication problems, love problems, and sexual problems. As real and painful and complex as these problems are, most of them can be resolved with the proper help. But the core issue is shattered covenants. In today's world, most people seem scarcely to understand covenants, much less to order their lives around them. People expect to stay married only as long as their mates provide what they want. Too few are willing to keep their covenants. Too few have the conviction to hang in there and give what their spouse needs for the marriage to last and flourish.

A godly spiritual leader is a covenant keeper in all his relationships, above all in marriage. Covenant-keeping in marriage assures the flock that this shepherd will also keep covenant with the flock of God, that he is going to be there, consistently, with the best interest of the church at heart—no matter what it costs him. The shepherd will "lay down his life for the sheep." He is not like the hireling who runs from trouble. He will not check out of the kitchen when the temperature rises.

The solidarity of an elder's marriage is a crucial leadership criterion because he and his wife will be mentoring marriage for countless others. Especially in our chaotic times, tenderhearted young people are on the hunt for healthy marital role models and for wise, personal counsel from successfully married older couples.

In this way, and many others, an elder's wife is his ministry partner. This is at least, in part, the reason Paul elaborated the qualities of wives in his character sketch of elders: "Their wives are to be women worthy of respect, not malicious talkers but temperate and trustworthy in everything."[11]

Success in His Relationship with His Kids

An elder's *relationship with his children* also calls for special attention. In fact, Paul zeros in on the parenting qualities of shepherds in both 1 Timothy 3:4–5 and in Titus 1:5–6. However, if Paul heard the way his words are sometimes applied today, he might protest, "That isn't what I meant." So glance back at these texts with me.

First, an elder is to have "children that believe." This does not imply, as some have suggested, that an elder must have more than one child. Paul is not even stressing the word "children" here—much less the *number* of children required. The grammar doesn't indicate such, nor does the context. The weight of Paul's point is that spiritual leaders' children must be *"faithful."*

Actually, the word "children" *(tekna* in the Greek) can be understood as either singular or plural, just as it can in English. For example: If I stand before five hundred modern Americans and say, "Would all of you with children please stand," those who have only one child would not likely remain seated, nor would this numerical specificity have occurred to Paul's audience in ancient times.

Of far greater significance than grammatical technicalities, however, is the nature and purpose of these character sketches.

Having *"children* that believe" is not meant as a test of *fertility* but as an indication of *spirituality,* of a man's skills at nurturing a healthy, faithful family.

Second, what does Paul mean by "a man whose children *believe"?¹²* Literally, the Greek says "faithful children." Some serious students of Scripture contend that this does not mean specifically that children be "faithful to *Christ";* rather, that Paul means they are to be faithful to their *parents!* The parents can trust them, and they respect their parents. That is, Paul may be thinking here not so much about shared religious beliefs as about successful, durable family relationships.

> ■
>
> Having
> *"children that*
> *believe"* is not
> meant as a test
> of *fertility* but as
> an indication
> of *spirituality.*
>
> ■

Third, the word *children* calls for some attention. The "believing children" are not little kids. "Children," in the extended family of Paul's world, included adult children. Note that this text describes children who are old enough that they could choose whether or not to be drinkers or "party animals." Paul's expression is "wild and disobedient."¹³ A "wild child," in this context, is obviously an *adult* child. So the question is not, "Did he get 'em baptized before high school graduation?" but, "Did he give them a faith that determines the way they live for a lifetime?" Obviously, little children at home do not provide the answer to that question.

Some might respond, "Well, Christian parents cannot be responsible for what their kids do after they become adults." True, "adult children" are free moral agents, responsible for their own behavior, and somewhere out there, the parental "statute of limitations" must run out.

Nevertheless, when Paul wrote that an elder's children must not be "disobedient," he did not intend to ask, "Can the man control the behavior of young children?" Of course, *little* children can be forced to obey us while they are still small enough that we tower over them physically. But we cannot force adult children to respect us and respond to us. Also, just because little children sing "Jesus Loves Me" does not mean they are believers in the sense Paul had in mind. He is suggesting that the grown children of an elder are to manifest an adult stability which *he* (their father) has fostered. Again, if an elder cannot inspire the love and respect of his adult children, why should he expect the love and respect of the church?

We are compelled to ask, "Why are children and parenting issues important to Paul?" Obviously, Paul believes a man's ability to build and maintain healthy relationships in his home provides evidence that he can do so in a church. He sees a strong connection between the spiritual leadership qualities of parents and the way their adult children live their lives. The durability of an adult child's faith is evidence of the authenticity of a parent's faith. And there is high correlation between an elder's ability to shape a "faith-contagious" environment in his home and his ability to do so in the church.

Warning: This children issue—while exceedingly important—can be pressed to unreasonable, legalistic lengths. Paul is not suggesting that an elder with four, balanced Christian children and one renegade is not qualified to be an elder. After all, adult children are free moral agents—fully capable of rejecting every good thing instilled by their parents. Neither is Paul suggesting that younger children acting out during adolescence disqualify a respected elder. Most people who have reared children to adulthood will understand that. So, the point of all of this can be summed up this way: look for men who, over the long haul, have produced stable, believing families. To drive home his point, Paul finally raises the powerful rhetorical question: "If anyone does not know how to manage his own family, how can he take care of God's church?"[14]

Experienced Lovers

Finally—yet of massive significance—Paul's character sketches for spiritual leaders picture elders who are experienced *lovers*. In fact, of all the qualities needed in an elder, "the greatest of these is love." A "wise ancient" in our congregation stopped me one morning after a message on spiritual leadership and quite emotionally asserted, "When it comes to selecting elders, if you ask me to choose between leadership and compassion, I'll take compassion every time."

We breathe an amen! The church will always need *leaders who are lovers*. When selecting elders—look for lovers.

Lovers of God

Good lovers, are first and foremost, people who love God. And good elders are men of prayer and praise. Oh, how God's church needs leaders who model persistent prayer, whose prayers glow with fervency, and who authentically believe God hears and cares. And how our spirits soar when leaders model vibrant praise and worship to God, who are unashamed to throw back their heads, open their mouths, and let their adoration—even their tears—flow in free and authentic worship. People who love God will also love people.

Lovers of the People of God

Besides being men who love God, good shepherds are men who love the *people of God.*

Modern-day Christians, like our ancient counterparts, are surrounded by competitive, self-serving, and intimidating pagans. This attitude so easily rubs off on us that we desperately need models of love. According to Scripture, good shepherds "lose sleep" over the flock. "They keep watch over you."[15] We love to rub up against those shepherds whose authentic love of people oozes through every pore. We feel comfortable taking our struggles to this kind of leader because he will not break our spirits, though we may have often broken his shepherd heart.

The best shepherd is approachable: warm and sensitive, not conceited, "not violent but gentle, not quarrelsome."[16] God's church needs leaders who care enough to know and feel what is going on in the life of this person or that, and who will listen, not with blank noncomprehending stares that seem oblivious to our feelings, but who lean in with attentiveness and tears—men who love.

> ■
>
> Good shepherds "lose sleep" over the flock.
>
> ■

I know first hand. I have personally received loving, soul-nurturing shepherding—many times. One particularly poignant day will stand out in my memory for a lifetime. An elder friend, whom I will call Joe, invited me to lunch. The invitation came during the darkest and most discouraging season of my ministry thus far. Yes, I had made some major blunders. But I had also been undermined and misrepresented for nearly a year by someone I had trusted as a friend. A series of coincidental mishaps ensued, escalating into an avalanche of misinformation. The whole debacle not only damaged my relationship with my shepherds, but shook my confidence. I felt overwhelmed with profound self-doubt about my ministry leadership skills—as if I were totally "losing it." In fact, I had even begun to question the validity of my forty years of ministry. And to add wallop, these events transpired during the last few months before I turned sixty.

Then came that pivotal afternoon with my dear friend Joe. First, over a leisurely lunch, Joe and I celebrated joys of grandparenthood and boasted to each other about our families. We shed real tears over shared heartaches and ministry breakthroughs.

> ■
>
> I felt overwhelmed with profound self-doubt about my leadership skills—as if I were totally "losing it."
>
> ■

Then, after lunch, we moved to a quiet place: Joe sensed I needed to talk. Joe listened to me pour out my hurt feelings, my sense of betrayal, the damage to my self-confidence. Then he brainstormed with me on a plan of action for "damage control."

Make no mistake, Joe shot straight with me all the way. But before he let me leave, he stepped over to the chair where I was sitting, placed his hands on my head, wept quietly for a moment, then prayed for me, and finally pronounced a blessing upon me.

I wept too, out loud—with release, yes—but with gratitude for the hands and the voice of a tender shepherd. I really needed a *loving* shepherd that day. That dear shepherd surely smelled like this sheep. His voice was clear and compelling, and I gladly put my life in his shepherd hands. In fact, even though I am no longer a minister of that church, nor even a member there, I have asked Joe to continue as my shepherd. Like all sheep, I need a shepherd who is a lover.

Lovers of People Who Don't Know God

Today's elders must be men of *the great commandment.* They are also called to be men of *the great commission.* Good shepherds are *lovers of people who don't know God.*

In Luke 15, Jesus told three interwoven stories that put us in touch with God's heart for lost people. One story is about a lost sheep—and a shepherd who left the flock in the open field and searched till he brought the lost one home "joyfully . . . on his shoulders."[17] Surely this shepherd smelled of sheep—*lost* sheep. The second story is about a woman who turned her house upside down to find a lost coin and then partied with her neighbors when she found it. The third story is the classic tale of the lost boy—and a father who longed for him to come home and threw a party when he did. All three stories loudly declare the over-whelming joy when the lost is found. Don't miss the punch line: "In the same way there will be more rejoicing in heaven over one sinner who repents than over ninety-nine righteous persons who do not need to repent."[18] Jesus weaves these three stories together to make one point clear: *lost people matter to God.* They are God's heart—his passion.

Lost people matter to God, and thus they matter to men of God. Hearts filled with the love of God will overflow with God's passion for lost people True, the main task of shepherding may not be looking for the lost: shepherds must take care of the saved. Yet, Scripture describes the heart of God as a shepherd with ninety-nine safe sheep, who left the safe ones and went looking for *one* that was lost.

Dr. Varner was an elder at the Highland Church when I first began ministry there. Everyone in town knew Dr. Varner. This tireless man had a busy medical practice and ran his own small hospital and clinic. He often dispensed spiritual prescriptions along with his pills. Although nearing retirement age and having many other responsibilities, Dr. Varner still found time to share the good news. Within one year, Dr. Varner brought more than forty people to Christ. So it comes as no surprise, when you run your finger down the ledgers recording the history of the Highland church, that the most militant and fruitful evangelistic years were on Dr. Varner's shepherding watch.

■

Lost people matter to God, and thus they matter to men of God.

■

Flocks usually take on the priorities of their shepherds. Elders who reach out to the lost generally build churches that reach out to the lost. Shepherds who don't evangelize attract flocks who don't either. Surely faithful shepherds search for the Father's *lost* sheep and teach the Word evangelistically. Good shepherds love people who don't know God.

Hospitable Lovers

Both 1 Timothy and Titus mention the quality of *hospitality*.[19] A hospitable man is not necessarily a "hale fellow well met" who slaps backs and drinks a lot of coffee down at Joe's diner. Rather, the biblical brand of hospitality seems centered around an elder's home. The word "hospitable," as used in Titus 1, technically meant, "hands open to strangers." But in the context of Paul's cultural setting, it more likely meant, "homes open to others." And the home of an effective shepherd is open often. Spiritual relationships with others deepen best as we gather in each others' homes. Some of the most beloved and effective shepherds I have known across the years live in homes that "smell like sheep." The quality of a shepherd's family life makes guests comfortable in his home.

When I was a mere lad of thirty-four, Carolyn and I moved away from eleven years of mission work in Canada, as I was called to the pulpit of a large church in Abilene, Texas. I soon realized I was in over my head. But those wonderful elders "took me to raise." One of the older elders in those days was Buddy Wade, long since gone home to Jesus. Carolyn and I spent our first few nights in Abilene at the Wades'. Later, across the years, we ate countless meals at Maureen's table. Our daughter, now a woman and a mother and a Christian leader herself, remembers how gracious and loving and "grandparent-like" Buddy and Maureen were to her.

> **Buddy held the man in his arms and wept as he prayed for the aged brother to feel secure in God's grace.**

Buddy Wade was a good shepherd. The whole church loved to hear him pray. Many were the late night crisis visits I made with brother Wade—and the hospital calls and home visits. For example, one time I walked into a hospital room with him where we visited an aged minister who lay under heavy conviction as he was setting his house in order to die. The sick man bared his soul to Buddy and me, confessing major personal sin. Buddy held the man in his arms and wept as he prayed for the aged brother to feel secure in God's grace. The warm heart of those warm Wade memories, however, always goes back to the living room of their house on Bird Avenue.

Clois and Betty Fowler, also represent the best in graciousness, hospitality, and shepherding. This shepherding couple is second grandparents to our grandchildren and many others. Their home is always a place of fun and hope and hospitality. I think now of many warm dinners around the fire at Clois and Betty Fowler's home. I remember laughing there, crying there, and praying there.

Few elders shepherd more college students than Dr. John Willis (Old Testament professor at Abilene Christian University) and his wife Evelyn, whose home is still crowded with young people nearly every Sunday night—and has been for over twenty years. This godly couple loves hospitality and works hard at it.

We receive only limited shepherding from elders whose living room couches and kitchen tables we have never seen, for these shepherds remain somewhat remote from us. When an elder has no place for me in his home, how can I feel he has a place for me in his heart? But when we go often to his home, we get a firsthand look at what goes on with his family, and we feel loved and valued by them.

My wife Carolyn and I share a passion for nurturing young ministers. For years, I have taught graduate ministry courses at Abilene Christian University, Pepperdine University, Preston Road Center for Christian Education, and other places. We deliberately limit enrollment, allowing plenty of time for personal interchange and class discussion. We end each semester (no matter what the course topic) with a three-hour seminar on marital stress peculiar to ministry families. The students and spouses or fiancées (if they have such) are invited to our home for dinner after the seminar. Then after dinner, Carolyn (and any of our kids that can be home at the time) fields questions for two or three hours, as the couples pick her brain about life in this minister's family—no holds barred, no questions off limits. The students invariably claim to get far more out of that home session than out of the class lecture. We have become firm believers in the power of spiritual leaders to open their homes and their lives to young couples and singles. The family circle is a most effective place to shepherd and mentor and equip the flock of God for useful family ministry. How do I know? The Bible tells me so—so do forty years of ministry.

> **The family circle is a most effective place to shepherd, mentor, and equip the flock of God for useful family ministry.**

Long experience at life, long experience at being a Christian, and the ability to be effective teachers of the Word are "musts" for spiritual leaders. However, these qualities alone do not necessarily make one an effective spiritual leader. All three—age, experience, and knowledge—must be tested in the crucible of family living.

In selecting spiritual leaders, we are not trying to find the "perfect" elder by meticulously checking off items on a check list. Rather, we are surfacing people who can most effectively shepherd, mentor, and equip our souls to honor God. As men are identified to be elders in God's church, let us watch for those who are mature, experienced teachers of the Word, who have reared healthy, believing families, and who are known as lovers. These men will be our best shepherds.

■

A follower of Jesus
Christ who seeks to
lead like Jesus must be
willing to be treated
like Jesus. Some will
follow. Others will
throw stones.

C. Gene Wilkes

CHAPTER

11

Men of Character

The apostle Paul's pastoral sketches spread before us in a collage of God-valued character traits. For purposes of brevity we gather them into three clusters: *consistency, self-control,* and *courage.*

Consistency

The elder profiled for Timothy and Titus is not perfect, but he *is* respected, or "above reproach."[1] This does not imply, "with no flaws and no critics." For, under even light scrutiny, we are all soon found flawed. And, amidst normal diversity, no one agrees with everyone. Plus, human pettiness and jealousy leave everyone disliked by someone—and what congregation does not include its share of naysayers. What Paul is saying, here, is that elders must be people who are *consistent* enough in character to earn the trust and respect of those who know them.

His character must be *respected,* says Paul, not just within the church, but "with outsiders" as well.[2] Of course, a man may be a big shot in the community, admired by the crowd, yet not remotely qualified for spiritual leadership. But on the other hand, when a man seems to be a big wheel in the church, yet the community at large holds him in contempt—watch out! After all, they may have his number. Jesus said something about the people of this world being "more shrewd in dealing with their own kind than are the people of the light."[3] Be ever so cautious about appointing him an elder.

An elder must not only be consistently respected to be a good shepherd, he must also be consistently *present.* Sheep can't flock a shepherd unless he is there—unstable shepherds create unstable sheep. How can a church follow a man who is erratic and unpredictable? But they will follow the *consistent* shepherd who can be trusted—day in, day out; year after year—to lead toward green pastures, still waters, and safe folds.

Control

Another strong ingredient of consistent character is *self-control.* Paul maps both negative and positive dimensions of self-control.

Negative Self-Control

Negative self-control leashes the dark side of human nature. It manages the volatile elements of one's own temperament.

First, a self-controlled person manages his *temper.* As Paul puts it, an overseer is "not overbearing, not quick-tempered, . . . not violent,"[4] and "not quarrelsome."[5] A violent or hot-headed man is no fit candidate for the shepherding role nor is the man who aims to "win by intimidation." Rather, a self-controlled shepherd is one who absorbs hostility, keeps his cool under attack, and returns good for evil. The late Carl Spain, a fine New Testament scholar, described this person as "the kind of man who doesn't settle arguments with his fists."[6]

Second, a shepherd-hearted man controls his *money*—rather than allowing his money to control him. A man who is preoccupied with money and forever scrambling to get more will not have the respect of God-hungry people, nor will people respect the values or trust the spiritual judgment of a leader who chronically battles careless debt. And a person whose financial irresponsibility leads him or her to shady business practices or questionable ethics is definitely in no position to proffer spiritual guidance. The self-controlled shepherd

■

"Negative" self-control leashes the dark side of human nature.

■

wants no part of "ill-gotten gain." He makes sure that his money is earned fairly and honestly. Money does not dominate him because he is driven by much larger values in his life: his heart is set on honoring God and serving people.

A few months back, some friends attended a small-town church one Sunday morning. Unfortunately, they found things numbingly irrelevant—*until* an elder came forward at the invitation song and tearfully confessed that he had filed bankruptcy. Apparently, he was one of the many casualties when the local economy hit the skids. He asked for prayers and said that, while he loved serving as one of the shepherds, in the light of his business reversals, he was resigning lest he "bring reproach on the church." My visiting friends came away deeply touched by this man's openness and by his heart. Now, if the man, indeed, was merely victimized by the economy, we might not agree that he needed to resign. But we would agree that his heart was right. He knew that even the slightest perception that he was not entirely aboveboard with money could mortally wound his spiritual leadership.

> People who are obsessed with looking for freedoms are not people with a heart for God!

Third, a man of spiritual-leadership caliber controls his *appetites*. Both Titus and Timothy were told that an elder shall not be "given to drunkenness."[7] The Greek *prosksontas paroinan* literally means one who is not "addicted to wine." As the late Dr. Carl Spain put it, "one whose mind is not turned to wine."[8] Most careful students of Scripture agree that Paul's references to wine are not a teetotaler's proof texts. And there is a vast difference between occasionally drinking wine and being addicted to wine. "Elders," it could be argued, "should have the same freedom to drink wine as any other Christian." True—given some social or cultural contexts. But let us say emphatically that people who are obsessed with looking for freedoms, especially those freedoms that could jeopardize the call of God, are not people with a heart for God! If an elder's cultural situation requires him to forgo his freedom to drink wine (or any other freedom for that matter) in order to have the trust of the church he leads, why would he insist on drinking? If a person values his or her freedom to drink wine more highly than the freedom to lead the church, that person is "given to" (addicted to) wine! Such a person may not be addicted in the sense that alcoholics anonymous defines addiction, but in the sense that the call of his or her freedom to drink wine is more compelling than the call of God!

If the marriage counselor says, "Okay, George, Mary says she cannot tolerate the amount of drinking you do. How little are you willing to drink in order to keep your wife and family?"

"Two beers a day!"

"Mary, can you live with that?"

"No."

"George. Are you willing to give up two beers a day to save your wife and family?"

"No."

What would you say about that man? He certainly appears controlled at least by his *freedom* to drink, if not by the drink itself. And whenever a person holds something personally more precious than service in God's family, something has gone dreadfully wrong. We flatly assert: that person is not fit for leadership in the body of Christ. Of course, this principle applies to the management of any appetite. The apostle Paul makes no bones about this, "It is better not to eat meat or drink wine *or to do anything else* that will cause your brother to fall."[9] The high calling of Christians is not to look out for our own interests[10] but "to serve one another in love."[11]

Positive Self-Control

Besides managing his temper, his money, and his appetites, a spiritual leader is to be in control of his *will*. Now we move to the positive dimensions of self-control. If "self-control"[12] means on the one hand that a person is to be in control of the volatile, *neg-*

ative elements of his or her nature, then on the other hand, *positive* self-control is to exercise "discipline."[13] In other words, an elder must exercise proactive self-management. Shepherding takes a lot of positive self-discipline. A shepherd takes positive action to be what the flock needs and to do what is best for the flock.

For example, exercise enthusiasts know it is difficult to jog regularly or to consistently maintain a workout regimen. To do so takes discipline. The person who exercises regularly, over the long haul, demonstrates "consistent discipline." Similarly, most busy people have to discipline themselves to spend the daily time in the Word that is needed just to *survive* spiritually—let alone

> ■
>
> An elder must
>
> exercise
>
> proactive self-
>
> management.
>
> ■

to lead and guide God's flock. Those who consistently flourish spiritually, despite eight to eighteen hours a day on the job, persevere only through discipline. They are positively self-controlled. *Discipline is the positive side of self-control.*

Many a faith shepherd, although battered by pain in his own life, consistently nurtures other hurting people. These are disciplined people—people of positive self-control. In fact, as my friend Wendell Broom says, "Most of the good that is done in this old world is done by people who don't feel like it at the time." Amen, Wendell. We hear you, Paul.

Stanley Scott, a faithful shepherd at my home church in Dallas, is in his late seventies. He is a retired senior partner from a nationwide accounting firm. Three years ago, he had bypass surgery. However, Stanley still works every day as a professional witness in civil litigation, traveling all over the nation on a schedule that would destroy a lot of people half Stanley's age. He also swims numerous laps every day and finds time to delight in his children and grandchildren. Yet Stanley rarely misses a shepherds' circle. And he and his wife, Toni, show up everywhere—at sickbeds, showers, dinners, concerts, new members' dinners, and more! And both of them appear to take full joy in all of it. Stanley is disciplined. He is one among thousands of faithful shepherds across the country who exemplify the highest in positive self-control.

Courage

In addition to being a man of consistency and self-control, the man of character is also a man of sterling *courage*. Paul calls him a "respectable" man.[14] He displays the courage to develop and pursue his own convictions. He makes his decisions based on his values rather than on pragmatism or mere expediency. He operates out of integrity and is driven by principle, not politics.

He is not threatened by group pressure or intimidated by pubic opinion. He is not swayed by hope of personal gain nor led astray by his own desire for prominence or power—not even by his own hunger to be liked—nor do his insecurities cause him to wither under fire. He is far more concerned about the needs of the flock than about avoiding criticisms from his denomination or his fellows. He will never, ever knowingly hurt an individual in order to ingratiate himself with the group.

This man of courage will likely want results, but he is no mere pragmatist. He does not follow the line of least resistance. He has established a track record of concern for precise biblical accuracy,[15] and he aims for what is spiritually beneficial for the family of God,[16] as well as what is strategic in reaching lost people. These matters concern him far more than doing what appears to be politically expedient. The shepherd of courage will unflinchingly do the will of God as he understands it, no matter what comes.

A man of character, bottom line, is a man who is authentic and who genuinely seeks to be God's man. This gives him the courage to do God's will and to love and serve God's people—no matter what it costs him personally.

Consistency. Self-control. Courage. Rare these days. But these are key character traits called for in Scripture and indispensable to the shepherds of God's flock.

> He makes his decisions based on his values rather than on pragmatism or mere expediency.

The first major shepherd of God's people, King David, was chosen for his character, which he actually learned among literal sheep. "From [shepherding] the sheep he brought [David] to be the shepherd of his people. . . . And David shepherded them with integrity of heart."[17] The hard life of the wilderness conditioned David as he *consistently* met hazards head on. Repeated confrontation with hostile elements drilled *courage* into his heart. Long, hard choices shaped his *self-control*. When danger threatened his father's sheep, he might just as easily have fled—his father would have been none the wiser. But David stayed and fought the lions and bears, even though no one was watching.

Character, after all, is best measured by what one does in a clinch, when no one else will know. In the absolute anonymity of the sheep pasture, when no one saw and no one knew, David repeatedly risked his life for a few stinking, stubborn sheep that could give him no personal rewards.

But God was his audience. And David's own heart was his supervisor. So he writes, "Search me, O God, and know my heart. . . . See if there is any offensive way in me."[18]

Our world is cynical. Even kids are wise to the duplicity of government leaders, televangelists, and Madison Avenue. Most folks desperately need to know a few good people who are straight shooters to the core. Schools need them—businesses too—and governments and kids. Most of all, the flock of God needs shepherds of authentic God-shaped character.

■

The most pathetic
person in the world
is someone who has
sight, but has no
vision.

Helen Keller

CHAPTER

Men of Vision

Today's churches need elders who are suited to the particular needs of their congregations—especially in our fast-changing, highly professional, excellence-oriented world. Here are some of the qualities that are needed in modern churches.

Visionary Leadership

First, while leading any church requires authentic men of God with true shepherding skills, most contemporary churches also need men of *vision*—men who will lead *boldly*, men who not only dream, but who have the "chutzpah" to transform dreams into reality. A church confronting the bustling market-place environment will likely flounder if waiting on plodders.

Most serious, twenty-first-century Christians want to forge ahead
to connect with and reach their changing culture. Many with this
spirit grow frustrated and leave congregations controlled by plodders who resemble the tour guide who is always the last one off
the bus, shouting, "Wait for me, I'm your
leader!" Today's church calls for leaders who
drive beyond their headlights and who
design churches for people "who aren't here
yet," rather than defending models
designed long ago to reach those who have
long since come and gone and who don't
live here any more.

■

Contemporary
churches need
men who not
only dream,
but who have
the "chutzpah"
to transform
dreams into
reality.

■

Our churches are desperate for visionary leaders who lead out with conviction
and with an eye to the future. We must not
resign ourselves to settle for what is; rather,
we must press on toward something better.
To paraphrase Robert Kennedy, "Most people see things as they are and ask, 'Why?' In
our day, we must see things as they could be
and ask, 'Why not?' " Our intent in this
book is not to describe the status quo, but
to excite dreams and encourage movement
into healthier and more biblical directions.

As overwhelming as this seems, we share the sentiment of William
Shakespeare, "Ah, but a man's dreams should exceed his grasp, or
what's a heaven for?"

Swiss mountain shepherds exercise unique visionary leadership with their flocks. In Switzerland, during the heat of summer,
the hot sun sometimes drains the lower valleys of moisture and
the grazing plays out. To provide healthy grazing and to keep
from losing the weak and the lambs, shepherds move their flocks

to the high country to graze in lush alpine meadows. To get there, however, they must climb precarious steeps through rugged rock. The older sheep resist. They feel secure where they are. Besides, they have done the hard trail and don't want to do it again. So the shepherds hoist the lambs to their shoulders and carry them up the hard trails to the high country. Of course, older sheep want to be near their young, and they trust those who care for the lambs. So eventually, in spite of the loss of the familiar and in spite of the hard climb ahead, the older sheep follow.

Today's spiritual shepherds who authentically care for their flocks sometimes face a similar dilemma. The survival of the flock, especially of the young and the weak, depends on some changes that older rams and ewes find painful. They resist. But if the shepherds are willing to "smell like lambs," if they will carry the young on their shoulders and boldly lead the way to the heights and the greener pastures, they can eventually gain a following from the older sheep. In many cases, this difficult adjustment may be the only way for the flock to flourish—even to survive.

It is not essential that all shepherds, however, be bold visionary leaders—that is, *if* they will give themselves to shepherding and delegate the bold, visionary leading to persons in their congregations who are visionaries with leadership gifts. In any case, today's churches stand in want of at least *some* visionary leadership.

Flexible Leadership

Today's churches also usually need elders who are *flexible*. Most churches in bygone days, and especially in more rural settings, have been quite homogeneous. They tended to be planted in communities where people all lived and looked much alike, where everyone drove Fords or Chevys, did similar things for a living, and tended to share similar values and a common world-view.

However, most of us don't live there anymore. Churches of our new environment call for at least some cross-culturally aware leaders who appreciate the force of today's pluralistic, ever-changing profile. Most church leaders confront a variety of educational backgrounds, age levels, cultural differences, socioeconomic strata, and even theological perspectives. What is more, contemporary churches—especially those in urban areas—are constantly adding new "constituencies." These churches need elders who discern the diverse worldviews this patchwork of constituencies brings to their pews. They will shepherd more effectively if they can stay in touch with the new issues and challenges that pluralism throws down in their path. In fact, some churches may even need a spectrum of different *kinds* of shepherds within one church. Then, in a pluralistic church, some of the elders may relate well to wealthy people, others to blue-collar people, while others may most effectively shepherd professionals; one shepherd relating to this ethnic background, another to that—all in the same congregation.

> ■
>
> Few of today's believers will be content to make their faith journey in a church whose leaders set the thing on auto pilot in the 1970s.
>
> ■

Our current technological and informational explosions also create fresh challenges for today's elders. The microchip has replaced the chalkboard in Christian education, e-mail the telephone, and the library is giving way to the Web. These are only the beginning. Shepherding in a fast-lane world calls for men who see exploding technology as a tool, not a threat.

The nineteenth century isn't going to happen again in the twentieth century—and we now stand on the threshold of the twenty-first century! Few of today's believers will be content to make their faith journey in a church whose leaders set the thing on autopilot in the 1970s and who have not been back to the cockpit since.

Welcoming Leadership

Now, more than ever, churches need leaders who are, or are willing to become, shepherds and equippers and who are not content to function merely as members of a "board of directors." Besides the fact that a board of directors is not a biblical model for church leadership, yesterday's styles of autocratic leadership simply won't work with today's people. Today's enlightened and empowered people will not be attracted to a church where they cannot own and determine some of the mission. This is, after all, compatible with the biblical concept of the "priesthood of believers."

Whether we like it or not, contemporary Christians shop from church to church, and neither congregational nor denominational loyalty will keep them coming back merely to sit on a pew—no matter how exciting the assemblies or dynamic the preaching. People don't want to be stuck in the status quo.

However, many *are* looking for life resources—for coping tools in the midst of life stress, for meaning and purpose, for hope and the feeling that things can get better, for authentic circles of relationships. So, in spite of "church shopping," the people most eager to grow spiritually will likely stay put and buy into a congregation that nurtures their spiritual growth and that of their families, that equips and empowers them to make a difference, and that offers them a place to genuinely belong. Their "church shopping" is more likely to end at the church that delivers *help, hope, and home.*

Thus, contemporary churches are best served by leaders who know how to assimilate people. Today's churches need elders who have the heart and know where to find the skills to enfold, nurture, equip, and empower people—men who either are doing these things now or demonstrate both desire and potential to grow into these roles.

Multiplying Leadership

To meet the growing hunger among Christians for hands-on shepherding, most growing churches simply must consider expanding their number of elders. After all, the idea of multiple shepherds per church is a very biblical notion, as Max Lucado points out:

> God never meant for the church to be a hierarchy with one person in charge. He never planned for a select few to perform all the ministry—he never intended for a certain few to do all the teaching or counseling. Ever since the resurrected Lord looked at Peter on the shores of Galilee and said, "Feed my sheep" (Jn. 21:15), there have been shepherds—overseers of the church dedicated to the task of leading, feeding, and the caring of sheep.[1]

Biblical models of leadership require a workable sheep-to-shepherd ratio. Healthy churches have enough shepherds to maintain authentic, intimate shepherd/flock relationships. Conceivably, this could mean one hundred shepherds in a twenty-five-hundred-member church, allowing for something like a twenty-five-sheep-to-one-shepherd ratio. Even the ratio of one to twenty-five might stretch things pretty thin.

You parents can understand what I mean. How would you like to parent twenty-five children, much less one hundred, five hundred, or a thousand? How can so many sheep receive biblical shepherding from one shepherd? Good shepherding means more pastors per sheep.

I can hear some dear reader groan, "Oh, my goodness, how could fifty or sixty elders meet together and make decisions? Won't a large numbers of pastors complicate the decision-making process and the efficiency of the meetings? My idea of an efficient elders' meeting is me and two other elders—with one of them sick and the other out of town!"

My experience says, "Yes. Admittedly, with a large number of elders, meetings could most definitely become exceedingly complicated!" So? The Bible doesn't charge shepherds with the responsibility of "having meetings." However, as we have noticed, Scripture *mandates* elders to shepherd, mentor, and equip the flock! Expanding the number of leaders in each congregation might impede corporate procedures, all right, but the shepherding and equipping potential would be vastly improved!

■

Healthy churches have enough shepherds to maintain authentic, intimate shepherd/flock relationships.

■

The operative question must not be, "What are we accustomed to?" but, "What does the Bible say?" Not, "What makes for efficient meetings?" but, "What makes shepherding effective?" Not, "What tidies up the schedule?" but, "What raises up the sheep?" After all, shepherding, mentoring, and equipping define the central biblical role of elders. Decision making, having meetings, and administrating—while they may have a place in implementing certain *minor* parts of the elder's role—do not constitute the biblical focus of God's calling for shepherds.

■

Expanding the number of leaders in each congregation might impede corporate procedures, but the shepherding and equipping potential would be vastly improved!

■

Think carefully about this, my friends. We may be robbing God's people of the very spiritual guidance so desperately needed in our times, when we actually replace *God's shepherd model* with our own *corporate model.* My dear brothers and sisters, please ponder this carefully: an ecclesiastical system that runs better when it sacrifices its biblical leadership function (shepherding, mentoring, equipping) to protect a nonbiblical function (efficient management and administration) cannot be of God! *Repeat: cannot be of God!*

Of course, elders need to meet at times. Ancient pastoral shepherds must surely have had some meetings, too. Out on the hillsides, where thousands of sheep were led by hundreds of shepherds, occasionally, no doubt, the shepherds would have to huddle and decide which pasture was overgrazed and who was to get what valley and who would go to what hill. Surely, they must have taken time to build common sheepfolds and clean out community waterholes. But our times call for elders who clearly see the difference between shepherding and administrating. If those ancient shepherds spent all of their time having meetings, their sheep would have wandered over the valleys and the hills, being devoured by the wolves. Rescue would grow ever more difficult as fewer and fewer sheep would recognize the voice of their shepherd! The task of a shepherd is to be out there with the sheep. Get a whiff of what that means—smell like sheep.

But having an adequately large number of elders surfaces another problem. As a friend pointed out to me recently, "Most churches may be willing to appoint an adequate number of elders, but feel it is not feasible because they face a critical shortage of mature men." Again, this merely describes the current status of churches. We must begin, *now,* working toward an expanding future that will not be limited by what is currently feasible. That is, more persons must be intentionally *matured.*

This is another compelling reason for church leaders to step up to another level as equippers and begin today instilling the skills necessary to fulfill that responsibility. Today is not a day too soon to begin devising and putting in place some means to get us there, to begin applying the biblical principles in the preceding chapters of this book.

Since we can see the enormous value—not to mention the biblical support—of an adequate ratio of shepherds to sheep, the sooner we begin putting that dream before churches the better. True, it may take a decade or more for a church to develop multiple mature elder candidates, but if churches don't begin that maturing process somewhere, sometime soon, those desperately needed shepherds will never mature—not even a century from now. To spin an old saw, "A thousand-mile journey begins with the first step."

Part of getting traditionally structured churches moving into a shepherd/flock direction is shifting the mental paradigm of church leadership, which this book attempts to do. Current church leaders can begin now to teach the biblical shepherd, mentor, and equipper models. They can begin to identify and dismantle hindrances to those models. They can implement vocabulary, structures, and practices in their congregations that shape a shepherding paradigm and foster fresh expectations about spiritual leaders.

Again, most strategic of all, Christian leaders must begin equipping—now! Otherwise, the best spiritual leaders will continue to burn out, growth will languish, and the initiative of many capable people, who could share the load, will be squelched or stymied. And the rest of the sheep will stray and starve.

Yes, oh yes, our times demand far more shepherds per sheep.

Delegated Leadership

Our times also call for spiritually discerning elders, who understand clearly the difference between *shepherding* and *administration*, between *managing* and *leading*. I acknowledge that this is ever so difficult to understand—given our history and the personality of our larger churches—but to effectively serve the people and faithfully honor God's design, leaders simply must move in the shepherding direction.

To be sure, managing and administration must happen. They are not four-letter words. But there are plenty of capable hands in most churches into which those chores can be passed. In fact, God has a design for that, too. Remember the problem that popped up early in the Jerusalem church when Greek-speaking and Hebrew-speaking widows generated a fight over food distribution? The church asked the apostles, "What are you going to do about this problem?" And the apostles replied, *"We* are not going to do anything. *You* are!" They told them to appoint seven deacons to sort out that organizational snafu and insisted that they stick with their shepherding priority.[2]

One may object, "Those men were not elders, they were apostles." True. But part of the function of the apostles at that point in the history of the church was to do what elders did later. First-century churches sometimes had deacons before they had elders, and for several reasons: (1) The church had not matured past the deacon level of spiritual leadership at that time. But as the church continued to grow, its leadership needs grew, too. It grew beyond simply managing the bucks, the bread, and bodies to become a visionary, caring, leading enterprise. (2) It took the early church a while to develop men who were gifted in teaching and spiritually mature enough to be ministers of the Word, like the apostles. At the time of the events described in Acts 6, it is unlikely that many people were yet qualified to shepherd. So, in a sense, the apostles were doing the shepherding of the Jerusalem church. (3) Aside from their inspired roles as "revealers," the apostles did shepherd work: spiritual formation, leadership, and teaching of the Word.

> ■
>
> Our times call for spiritually discerning elders who understand clearly the difference between shepherding and administration.
>
> ■

Today, most congregations need more shepherds, not more administrators. In many cases, we have capable—but unchallenged and unused—administrators running out our ears, who could "lift a lot of load" off our elders and free up elders to shepherd, mentor, and equip.

However, the pragmatic church of the twentieth century tends to be more aware of the practical and visible "deacon issues" in many settings. Thus, the relentless undertow of the system subtly tugs elders into these "deacon" things, leaving them little time to deal with the far more important "shepherding issues." There may have been a place in simpler, smaller times for elders to both administrate and shepherd—and do both effectively. But not any more. In our complex times, the challenge grows increasingly difficult for the same men to both shepherd and administrate well. Time to revive the biblical mode is past due.

> ■
>
> Today's elders must be willing to delegate their current non-shepherding tasks to others.
>
> ■

Today's elders must be willing to delegate their current nonshepherding tasks to others. After all, why must elders be the ones who manage the money when there are professional bankers and accountants among the deacons? Why must elders plan construction projects and run maintenance crews when capable deacons would love the job, and in many cases could do it just as well or better? One minister commented,

> I have been a part of too many meetings that were totally consumed with discussion about the bad roof, etc. One meeting recently is typical of too many others: We all left the meeting room and walked downstairs to look at a wall that was wet because of a leaky pipe—tying up several precious shepherds for more than thirty minutes. That same night some Christians sat in their homes in the dark, with their heads in their hands—gasping for "spiritual air," longing for shepherding. All the while, some capable

deacons would have loved the building maintenance job but stayed frustrated because they didn't know what was expected of them.

It might be interesting to probe into the psychology behind the tendency of some elders to focus on issues like insurance, the roof, or a leaky pipe. One wonders, Is it a fundamental misunderstanding of the ministry of shepherding? Or does doing these kinds of things give them the feeling that they *at least* accomplished *something?* Could the wrong men be attempting to serve as shepherds?

And why must elders sort out organizational and personnel issues, when there are professional management consultants on the pews? Today, more than ever, elders absolutely must be willing to delegate nonshepherding tasks to deacons and others. This is no small issue, belonging in the fine print on the back of the bulletin or among the in-house church humor. It is front-burner stuff. Churches simply must return to a more biblical and workable model, if the shepherds are ever to be freed up to shepherd!

Most flocks these days hunger to be fed by spiritual shepherds. They need more hands-on guidance than they did back in simpler days. They long for leaders to equip them and shepherds to lead on over the mountains. The heart of the Chief Shepherd longs for this as well!

Hostility-Absorbing Leadership

Today's churches are filled with varying perspectives and tastes, which means leaders cannot please all of the people much of the time. In addition, people in our day demand—I say *demand*—excellence. For example, the bumper-sticker slogan of our local high school team insists, "Nothing Less Than Perfection." Actually, this sticker screams the mindset of my Dallas Park Cities community in all areas of life—including what they expect from the church. In this kind of culture, an imposing segment of the people will not be pleased even with the best efforts of the finest leaders. Consequently, thin-skinned, easily swayed, insecure persons won't lead well or last long. Today's spiritual leaders must be able to put criticism in proper perspective. They must be *good listeners* on the one hand and *clear thinkers* on the other. Above all, they must be able to absorb hostility—regularly and over the long haul, becoming neither hardened and insensitive, nor bitter, angry, and defensive. This challenge demands great strength of character and the emotional health that flows out of peace with God.

■

Thin-skinned, easily swayed, insecure persons won't lead well or last long.

■

For shepherds to attempt to please every self-appointed expert is a foolish and unbiblical notion. Yet we hear these sentiments, "Everyone *is* important you know . . . and we *are* on call twenty-four hours a day . . . and we *do* live in a fishbowl—like it or not."

A sincere sounding but subtly misguided form of servant-heartedness believes that the spiritual leaders must serve the demands of all the church people. But Paul didn't see it that way. He said of spiritual leaders, "Men ought to regard us as servants of Christ."[3] The "servant" word here is *huperetas,* or "under-rowers," a metaphor drawn from the slaves chained to the oars in the ship's galley. Orders from the captain—and no one else—marked out the rhythm of the oarsmen's strokes. Imagine what confusion and frustration would result if the galley slaves attempted to take their orders from the cacophony of tourists' voices on the deck?

The oars would become hopelessly tangled, and the boat would fall behind the rest of the convoy. Stress would mount. The oarsmen would become demoralized, out of touch with the captain's wishes, and envious of the ships who were passing them up. Spiritual leaders are, indeed, servants—but they are servants of Christ! He alone calls the signals and sets the pace.

Listen to Paul drive home his point: "My conscience is clear. . . . It is the Lord who judges me. . . . He will bring to light what is hidden in darkness and will expose the motives of men's hearts. At that time each will receive his praise from God."[4]

Repeat: Who is the master? Christ! Shepherds serve people best when their hearts long most deeply for the glory of God. Jesus even said, "How can you believe [if you] receive glory from one another and do not seek the glory that comes from the only God?"[5] When their activities flow out of the will of Jesus rather than from a need to maintain favor with the whole church, shepherds will find their own work both less stressful and more fruitful. Otherwise, few leaders will survive pluralistic churches in our fast-lane world.

Need Only the Perfect Apply?

A final word of caution on "qualities": remember, the qualities of elders in Scripture are character sketches, not legal checklists. Beware, lest a rigid and idealistic misuse of them makes us hypercritical of the imperfections of our leaders. Deal lovingly, lest we create impossible expectations that only set our leaders up for failure.

The Bible sketches an absolute ideal. However, in the real world, we are constrained to settle for the leadership of flawed human beings. Thus, with these biblical character sketches in hand, let us recognize those in our congregations who, in spite of

■

Let us recognize those in our congregations who most resemble the experience and character sketched in Scripture.

■

imperfections and shortcomings, most resemble the experience and character sketched in Scripture. In reality, the "best we have" will be leading the faithful anyway, whether we officially call them elders or not. Indeed, they usually are recognized as shepherds—if not officially, then unofficially.

Beyond all this, healthy churches are made up of those who follow Jesus, no matter what we think of the leaders in the church. Most of us, rather than being critical of our leaders would be better served by learning to be and do what we expect our leaders to be and do. In the final analysis, it is the Chief Shepherd to whom we look for guidance as we share this responsibility and privilege together.

Section Two:

Authority

■

Sometimes *pastors* become *pastures*. The sheep feed on them and trample them, but do not follow them.

Mark Absher

CHAPTER

The Biblical Language of "Authority"

When I was ten, Raymond used to bully me. He loved to hit me with vicious names like, "scaredy-cat," "crybaby," or "sissy." Don't tell him, but I was terrified of Raymond. Of course, I tried to sound as confident as John Wayne, as I shot back my defense, "Sticks and stones may break my bones, but words will never hurt me." Trouble is, deep down I knew I wasn't telling the truth. Actually, Raymond's words hurt a lot. Of course, most of us log a few visible scars on the outside from the tangible "sticks and stones," but those are nowhere nearly as hurtful as the internal scars left by words. Words can inflict a lifetime of painful memories and damaged self-esteem.

Words can hurt churches, too. In fact, some unfortunate vocabulary has inflicted long-term damage to our understanding

187

of spiritual leadership—words like *rule, authority, submit,* and *obey.* These words are especially damaging if we are among those who feel obliged to unquestioningly obey and submit to the complete authority of those in the "office" of elder/bishop/pastor.

■

Some unfortunate vocabulary has inflicted long-term damage to our understanding of spiritual leadership— words like *rule, authority, submit,* and *obey.*

■

These bruising words didn't come from the Bible, however. That language was actually coined by seventeenth-century Anglican ecclesiastical tradition and was passed on to us through the King James translators. Paradigms of church polity and gut feelings on the subject of ecclesiastical authority—which have been shaped by those translators' imprecise and sometimes downright distorted vocabulary—have left internal scars on the twentieth-century church. So, in the next few pages we shall attempt to peel away the faulty definitions of some "elder role" words and more nearly recover their New Testament meanings.

what Is "Office"?

It may come as a surprise to some, but the Greek New Testament never refers to spiritual leadership as an "office." The King James Bible translates 1 Timothy 3:1, "If a man desires the *office* of a bishop, he desireth a good work." The word *office* derails our thinking in at least two ways: (1) It sends our minds down the path leading to an institutional paradigm of the church—so alien to the organic paradigms of the New Testament.

(2) The "office" concept postures elders as agents of institutionalized authority—so alien to the shepherd, mentor, and equipper models of the New Testament.

Biblically speaking, *bishop (elder, shepherd)* is a function, not an office; a task, not a position. This phrase in 1 Timothy 3:1 might more accurately be translated, "if anyone *desires to bishop."*

What Is "Bishop"?

Probably no word has played a greater part in shaping opinion about the function of elders as leaders than the term *episkopos,* or plural, *episkopoi,* translated "bishop(s)" in the King James Version. The word appears four times in the New Testament,[1] translated by various versions as "bishop," "overseer," "superintendent," and "guardian." However, as Dr. Carl Holladay of Emory University comments, "Further examination into the word and its background makes one wonder if such renderings do not say more about the translators than about the original meaning of the word."[2]

The word *bishop,* like the word *office,* carries an authoritarian aura from the seventeenth century into the modern church. However, this is not at all the New Testament meaning of the word *episkopos.* It could be more fully translated "guides," "those who watch out for," "those who are concerned on behalf of," or "those who care for" the church—but not those who *"rule over"* it.

In ancient, secular Greek literature, the verb *episkopeo* is used in the sense of "to look upon," "to consider," "to have regard for something or someone."[3] At times it referred to the Greek gods' watching over the treaties of human beings. Greek ship's captains were described as the *(episkopoi)* "overseers" of the cargo.

But, while early on, *episkopeo* expressed acts of protection or watch-care, later it also meant "to visit," as in visiting the sick.

This latter meaning seems to have been "baptized" from secular Greek into biblical usage.

Beyer explains: "It *(episkopoi)* combines the various senses of "to visit, to look upon, to investigate, to inspect, to test, to be concerned about, to care for."[4] For example: In the Septuagint (Greek Old Testament), the word *episkopos* describes what Samson did when he went to visit his wife (to care for her). Several examples of this idea show up in the Old Testament.[5] And the Greek Old Testament frequently uses the word *episkopeo* or *episkopos* to describe what a *shepherd is doing when he cares for his sheep!*[6] Zechariah even describes the bad shepherd as one who "does not care for *(episkopos)* the perishing."[7]

> ■
>
> As if to make clearer that bishops are not rulers, the apostle Peter warns them not to "lord it over the flock."
>
> ■

Bingo! Where have we heard this before?

In the New Testament, the word *episkeptomai* expresses a fundamental Christian teaching: that each of us exists for the other. Jesus taught us to care for one another, and James said we are to "look after" orphans and widows, describing this as "pure and faultless" religion.[8] Therefore, we love one another and submit to one another, each considering others better than himself.[9] In that connection, the word *episkeptomai* meant more specifically "to seek out someone," not merely "pay him a visit." It implied a sense of responsibility and concern toward that person.[10] Furthermore, it points up the responsibility of all of the members of the *community of faith* to take care of one another. For example, the word *episkopeo* is used to mean "look out for" (search for) men to care for the neglected widows.[11] The basic idea is "concern and care for one another." Again, as Dr. Holladay puts it, "To the extent that this relational definition is pushed into the background, to that extent the New Testament impact of *episkopos* is lost."[12]

Strikingly, the New Testament "marries" the word *episkopos* *(bishop)* to the word *shepherd (poimaino),*[13] when referring to elders. Bingo again! The duties of the "overseer" are described in shepherding or pastoral (pasture) terms. As if to make clearer that bishops (elders) are not *rulers,* the apostle Peter warns them not to "lord it over" the flock.[14]

We conclude, then, that the sentiment of 1 Timothy 3:1 might be more accurately expressed in something like the following words: "If anyone wants to be concerned about and care for a church, he desires something excellent." "Office" of elder—in its bone-breaking, authoritarian, and institutional sense—is not what Paul had in mind when he wrote Timothy about spiritual leaders.

what Is "Rule"?

But, someone objects, "What of Paul's words, 'Elders who *rule* well' are worthy of 'double honor'?"[15] At this point we are hit by another bone-breaking word, which is often mistranslated— and consequently misapplied. The word *(proistotes,* a form of *proisteemi)* is translated in the King James Version as "rule." However, the word *rule* comes from seventeenth-century religious context, not from the New Testament. The New International Version renders *proistotes* as those "who *direct the affairs* of the church."

Granted, classical Greek did use the word *proisteemi* in some settings meaning "to be set over" or "to be the chief power"—as of Hellas or Arcadia—or more commonly "to be at the head of a party" or "to act as chief or leader."[16] In the Septuagint, this word is used several ways. It describes the "young man who *served*" Amnon,[17] the *"stewards* of King David's property,"[18] "the *chief officers* of King Solomon . . . who *exercised authority* over the people,"[19] and others.

On the basis of the ancient usage, some commentators of years gone by supported the King James New Testament translation of *proisteemi* as "to rule" when it describes the elder's task.[20] However, while such use may be found in classical usage and the Septuagint, the important questions for this study are: How is *proisteemi* used in the New Testament? What does it mean for the elders to *proisteemi?*

In the New Testament, the verb form is used eight times—all by Paul. The noun form *prostatis* is used but once. And the word *proisteemi* is employed in several ways.

First, in Romans 12:8 the King James Version translates *proisteemi* as "he that ruleth, with diligence" (referring to one of the seven spiritual gifts). But the Revised Standard Version translates it "he who gives aid, with zeal." The New International says, "if contributing to the needs of others, let him give generously." Apparently, at least some noted scholars feel that *proisteemi* in Romans 12:8 means "to care for or be concerned about," not "to lead or to guide."[21]

Second, in Romans 16:2, the lady Phoebe grabs our attention. Very significantly, this word is used to tell us that Phoebe, a "deaconess" of the church, has been *prostatis* (the feminine noun form of *proisteemi)*—a "helper" (RSV), "a great help" (NIV), to Paul and others. Surely this does not mean that Phoebe *ruled* the church! Nor does Paul's use of this word imply that elders rule the church.

A third use of *proisteemi* appears in 1 Timothy 3:4–5 in a family setting. Paul says that an elder is to "manage his own family well" (NIV) or to "rule" his family (KJV). Deacons are to do the same.[22] But, in this same context Paul uses a different word for the elder's role in the church. The elder is to "manage" *(proisteemi)* his family, but he is to "take care of" *(epimeleomai)* (RSV, NIV) the church. "If anyone does not know how to manage *[proisteemi]* his own family, how can he take care of *[epimeleomai]* the church of God?" True, the term *proisteemi* in a father-child relationship will nurture submissive and respectful children, but not because it implies arbitrary authority in the parents. Rather, such children are the product of fathers who provide for their family and truly care for them.[23]

> Surely this does not mean that Phoebe *ruled* the church! Nor does Paul's use of this word imply that elders rule the church.

Fourth, let us note another dramatic use of this word. Our word *epimeleomai* describes the care given a robbery victim in the story of the Good Samaritan. In that story, the "caring for" is crystal clear. When the good Samaritan pays the innkeeper to "look after" *(epimeleomai)* the robbery victim,[24] he is obviously not asking the innkeeper to "rule over" the man. Nor is he asking the victim to "submit to and obey" the innkeeper. Rather, the Samaritan is asking the innkeeper to "take care of, give aid to" the robbery victim. Why then should this same word mean that an elder is to rule the church? Rather, he is to care for the church in a manner equivalent to the Good Samaritan's care for the robbery victim.

Finally, in Titus 3:8 and 14, the context makes it abundantly obvious that *proisteemi* means to "busy oneself with" or "to apply oneself to" good works, rather than "to rule."

We conclude, then, that *proisteemi* in 1 Timothy 5:17 does not imply "ruling" elders and "obeying" members. Rather, the biblical understanding of *proisteemi* is far more compatible with the shepherd-mentor-equipper metaphors (which we explored in previous chapters) than with the idea of ruling authority figures. Elders are not those who rule the flock from the clout of an "office." They are shepherds who care for the flock and who smell like sheep. The lead-up context of 1 Timothy 5:17 is about works of compassion—specifically the care of widows—and about service. And the "service" idea is further underscored as Paul advises Timothy that those men who thus "direct the affairs of the church" are worthy of double honor—*especially* if they "work in preaching and teaching."

what About 1 Thessalonians 5?

Paul's charge to the Christians of Thessalonica, delivered via the King James Version, has been viewed in former decades in light of an authority/submission paradigm: "know them which labour among you, and are over you in the Lord." This verse has been interpreted as meaning that members of the congregation are to be subservient to its elders. However, when we read 1 Thessalonians 5:12–13 in the New International Version and actually view it in context, we get a very different idea: "We ask you, brothers, to *respect* those who work hard among you, who are over you in the Lord and who admonish you. *Hold them in the highest regard in love* because of their work." Properly rendered, this sentence does not assault our ears with the clang of authoritarianism and subservience, but sings softly of a relationship of love and respect between leaders and those being led, between caregivers and those being cared for.

Are These Guys Elders?

Who are these men who are to be the object of our respect and affection? A panoramic sweep of Paul's Thessalonian letters explains. They are described three ways: First, Paul refers to the ones desiring respect as "those who work hard among you,"[26] reminiscent of Paul's own physical toil and evangelistic efforts as he "worked night and day in order not to be a burden to anyone"[27] while he preached the gospel.

Second, those to be respected are called those "who are over you in the Lord."[28] Remember, this is our word *proisteemi,* which, as discussed earlier in this chapter, means "to care for," "give aid," and "serve." It is doubtful, however, that this passage is specifically about elders. Elders are not mentioned elsewhere in the Thessalonian correspondence, whereas they are mentioned in Paul's other epistles. First Thessalonians is one of the earliest, if not the very earliest, of the New Testament letters. So it is unlikely that the Thessalonian church even had elders at this time. Since it was young, the church at Thessalonica may have been developing through a time of informal and voluntary leadership, as do most "church plants." As Dr. Neil points out, "Not until about ten years later, in his letter to the Philippians, did Paul make his first clear reference to the official order of elders and deacons."[29]

> ■
>
> Paul refers to the ones desiring respect as "those who work hard among you."
>
> ■

Furthermore, elders are not the only persons whom Christians are to "respect" and "hold in esteem." Epaphroditus, for example, a fellow worker of Paul, was to be "honored" for his service.[30] Actually, Christians are told to "submit" to *"everyone* who joins in the work, and labors at it."[31] And Moulton and Milligan, as well as Hort, explain in reference to this Thessalonian passage, that the word *proisteemi* can also imply levels of rank within a congregation.[32]

Third, those to be respected are called those "who *admonish* you."[33] Mutual admonition among the Christian community seems to have been a fairly common practice.[34] Apparently, the admonitions of the leaders were being neglected by some (perhaps the lazy folks at Thessalonica), and this put a strain on the relations between them and the spiritual advisors, but we need not infer that these advisors were elders of the church.[35]

So it seems that the people Paul urges these Thessalonian Christians to respect are most likely those *informal leaders who served and helped the church at Thessalonica.* In this light, the second part of Paul's statement makes more sense, "Hold them in the highest regard in love *because of their work,*" not because they "rule over you." Clearly, the warm verb *eidenai* carries the fitting sentiment of love and respect here, not the sonorous "obey" of the King James Version.

> ■
>
> To construct a system of elder authority "by right of office" is to misuse the text.
>
> ■

Of course, respect for leadership "because of their work"[36] is expected by this passage—and throughout the New Testament—but to construct a system of elder authority "by right of office" from these phrases is to misuse the text. It also creates an environment of "sticks and stones" that threatens the health of our "bones." Oh yes, these authoritarian words can "hurt us."

whew! More Big words! "power,"
"Authority," "leaders"

Three more important, big words come in this cluster: *exousia* and *timee,* or "power" and "authority"; and *eegoumenois,* or "leaders."

The first two of these words need only to be pointed out: *exousia* and *timee.* These are the precise words the Greeks routinely used for "authority" and "power." And here is our point: significantly, these two words are *not used in the New Testament in connection with elders!*

This brings us to our third "authority word"—*eegoumenois (leaders).* This word, like some other "authority" words, is used in both classical Greek and in the Septuagint to denote men in leading positions or even rulers.[37] But in the New Testament, this word is used with several different meanings. The leader *(eegoumenos)* is "one who serves."[38] Stephen called Joseph a "governor" *(eegoumenos)* over Egypt.[39] Paul's eloquence set him off as "chief speaker" *(eegoumenos).*[40] Judas and Simon are chosen as "leaders men among the brothers" *(eegoumenoun)* and trusted to bear a letter to Antioch.[41]

In Hebrews 13:17 and 24 this word *eegoumenois* appears three times with reference to leaders in the church. The King James Version has the writer saying three things about leaders of the church:

1) "Remember them which have the rule over you" *(eegoumenoi,* v. 7).

2) "Obey them that have the rule over you *[eegoumenoi]* and submit to their authority" (v. 17).

3) "Salute all them that have the rule over you" *(eegoumenoi,* v. 24).

What about these three phrases?

First, the only common denominator among these uses of *eegoumenoi* is that in each case the leaders in some way stood out from the rest of their respective groups, but there is nothing to necessarily imply that these leaders were elders. "Leaders" may refer simply to "outstanding brethren" who do not hold any official "office" in the church. Elders are not specifically named.

Second, when Jesus contrasted godly leadership, "one who serves," with the authoritarian style of worldly leaders who "exercise lordship and authority," he stated flatly, "I don't want you leading like the pagans!" Or more specifically,

> The kings of the Gentiles lord it over them; and those who *exercise authority* over them call themselves Benefactors. But *you are not to be like that.* Instead, the greatest among you should be like the youngest, and the one who rules like the one who serves.[42]

Surely the Hebrew writer would not tell these leaders, whoever they were, to do exactly opposite to what Jesus so clearly commanded.

Third, as we have already noticed, this word *eegoumenois* is not ordinarily used in connection with authoritarianism in the New Testament but could well be translated "taking the lead."

■

When Jesus contrasted godly leadership with the authoritarian style of worldly leaders, he stated flatly, "I don't want you leading like the pagans!"

■

Hooray! The Last Big Words: "Obey" and "Submit"

Finally, the readers of Hebrews are also told to "obey" *(peisesthe)* and to "submit" *(hupeiko).*[43]

First, this respect is to be paid because "these leaders keep watch over your souls . . . joyfully." This respect grows out of a healthy relationship with the leaders who lead Jesus style.

Second, if this passage *does* refer to elders (although we think it does not), it still does not enjoin obedience to them. As noticed earlier, other passages show that Christians are to *mutually* respect one another. For example, see 1 Corinthians: "Submit to such as these" *(upotasso),* who devoted themselves to the service of the saints, "and to *everyone* who joins in the work."[44] Actually, mutual submission is a universal and bedrock principle of the Christian faith.[45] But submission cannot be demanded *from* another. Rather, by its very nature, it is offered *to* one another, nor does Paul's instruction on mutual submission license one to be an authority figure over another. This principal of mutual submission obligates none of us to subservience or blind obedience before any human being. Rather, the words *peisesthe* and *hupekete* urge an attitude of loving service and respect for one another.

So . . . ?

Having looked a bit more carefully at the major descriptive New Testament terms for elders and other words relating to leadership and our attitudes toward one another, we reach these conclusions:

First, elders definitely carry leadership responsibility. However, only with great reluctance should this leadership be called "authority" since the usual Greek "power" words, *exousia* and *timee,* are never used in connection with elders.

Second, godly leadership is to be understood in terms of service rather than authority. Jesus is adamant on this point.

Third, the term *proisteemi,* describing the leadership of shepherds, is best translated "to care for" or "to give aid." To translate it "rule" obscures and distorts the original meaning.

> ■
>
> Only with great reluctance should this leadership be called "authority."
>
> ■

Fourth, the two passages often used to "prove that a congregation must submit to the authority of the elders" likely do not refer specifically to elders at all. At best, Hebrews 13:17 and 1 Thessalonians 5:12–13 supply an exceedingly flimsy foundation on which to build authority for the "office" of elder or to argue that elders command obedience. However, these passages do teach that all Christians, including elders, are to respect and submit to each other. Respect, however, is something chosen by the one who does the respecting, not demanded by the one respected! Only Jesus holds *"all authority."*[46]

When elders rely on their "authority" and "rank" to achieve a following, they may be exercising leadership of a sort, but definitely not at all the type of spiritual leadership the New Testament describes.

Fifth, a warning: let us not, therefore, jump to the conclusion that elders have *no* authority. Good shepherds carry enormous authority, but it is the authority of *moral suasion,* not of rank. And let us never assume that since we are not *mandated* to obey, this somehow means we need not respect spiritual leaders. Elders are to be respected just as the other leaders of the Christian community; indeed, far more so, because of their maturity in the faith, their character, love, and work. And, because the flock has asked them to shepherd.

Words That Won't Break Bones

The words Scripture most commonly uses for spiritual leaders—elders, pastors, bishops—are clearly not "office" words or "authority" words. Rather, they are descriptive words, describing the relational nature of spiritual leadership.

Remember, elders *(presbuteroi)* simply means "older" or "leaders." Pastors *(poimaenoi)* are simply "shepherds." And bishops *(episkipoi)* can accurately be translated as those "who watch out for," "who are concerned on behalf of," or "who care for" the church.

Rather that fixating on the bone-crushing words used earlier, let us scan, instead, the beautiful, soul-nurturing, relationship-building functions God has in mind for spiritual leaders. Read them slowly, carefully, reflectively. Ponder their rich, deep beauty:

- Keep watch (guard), oversee, shepherd [47]
- Take care of God's church [48]
- Direct affairs, preach, teach [49]
- Encourage, refute falsehood [50]
- Pray over and anoint the sick [51]
- Shepherd the flock, serve God's flock, be examples to the flock [52]
- Prepare God's people for works of service [53]

Here's another way to detail the leader's functions:

- Shepherd the flock
  - Teach them

- Touch them
- Protect them
- Lead them
- Teach the Word
  - Feed them
  - Encourage them
  - Refute false teachings dangerous to them
- Guard the flock (from spiritual dangers)
- Lead the flock
- Care for the flock (maintain, oversee, be watchful on behalf of)
- Serve the flock
- Be examples to the flock
- Preach the Word
- Pray for the flock
- Anoint the sick and pray for them
- Direct the affairs of the flock
- Take thought for the flock
- Busy oneself with the flock
- Lose sleep over the flock
- Equip the flock for ministry

Notice that the authority/obedience syndrome is conspicuously absent from the spirit of this amalgam profiling biblical spiritual leadership.

The remote and controlling style of some modern church leaders who operate as sheriffs or CEOs runs completely counter to the Almighty's arrangment. In some instances—at its worst—the authority-office-rule approach has resulted in one or more of the following:

- Controlling the flock
- Withholding from or granting permission to the flock
- Managing the money and administrating the facilities donated by the flock
- Setting corporate policy for the flock
- Determining the worship styles of the flock (even setting time limits on their worship)
- Bossing the ministers of God or micromanaging the various ministries and activities of the flock, thereby, suppressing the energy and creativity of the flock
- Greasing the squeaky wheels of the flock
- Maintaining the status quo of the flock
- Taking the flock to those pastures (or was it deserts?) desired by the powerful rams and elegant ewes (especially the loudest bleaters), regardless of the wishes and best interests of the rest of the flock
- Fleecing the flock
- Having meetings—many meetings, long meetings, unnecessary meetings, private meetings— away from the bleating voices, up-turned faces, hungry souls, and smelly carcasses of the flock

■

These bruising words have steered us away from the joy and health of God's design for leadership.

■

And on the list could go on.

What stark contrasts between the biblical portrait of spiritual leaders and some modern church leadership. Sticks and stones may break our bones, but words? These "authoritarian/obedience" misuses of beautiful biblical functions, relationships, and attitudes have indeed dealt many of us a world of hurt. They have rolled out the welcome mat to interlopers who would rule with ungoldy authority. And for at least a century, these bruising words have steered us away from the joy and health of God's design for leadership revealed in Scripture.

Ah, but the real authority of elders! Now that is something wonderful. Read on!

■

An elder who has to *assert* his authority usually doesn't have much.

Lawrence Anderson

The Authority of Moral Suasion

In the previous chapter we have pointed out that there is no such thing as the "office" of elder in the Bible. (The term "eldership" is not a biblical term either.) We also noted that the notion of authority and obedience do not fairly represent the letter, much less the sentiment, of the actual New Testament language. These observations may trigger the question, "Well, does this mean elders have *no* authority?"

Our answer is "Yes and No. Definitely!"

Yes

First, yes. Yes, this means elders have no authority in the institutional, traditional "ecclesiastical office-holder" sense. The elder does not metaphorically wear a badge, carry a gun, or take

charge. And those who attempt this deserve no respect or followers and will receive little of either. As my father used to say,
"When a person needs to 'assert his authority,' it usually means he
has very little of it."

■

The elder
does not
metaphorically
wear a badge,
carry a gun, or
take charge.

■

We have observed from the original
language that the New Testament does not
place elders "over" other Christians, nor are
the rest of us obliged to "obey" simply
because "the elders said so." Biblically, the
authority of an elder is not of position, but
of *moral suasion*. We have also noted, of
course, the well-established Christian principle that Christians are to respect and submit to one another.[1] This respect obviously
includes Christian's spiritual leaders, but
the New Testament does not call for "obedience" to another Christian simply
because he "holds an office."

No

Second, no. No, this does not mean that elders are without
authority—quite the contrary. The biblically shaped shepherd—
a Christ-imitating elder—holds enormous moral suasion. In fact,
so much so that his sheep will hear his voice and no other. They
will follow him as he follows Jesus, as he goes "in and . . . out and
find[s] pasture."[2] Shepherds and mentors who build credibility by
service, warm relationships, and a consistent display of a winsome
and lasting faith-walk need not *assert* authority, for they hold
immense influence in our lives.

My father held no political, economic, physical, or organizational authority over me. But he lived his life well, loved me,

served me, cared for me, and walked ahead of me in the Lord. And I most assuredly respected and submitted to his suggestions for my life. Truth is, Dad has great authority over me—even though he went to heaven six years ago. And there are a number of other godly men and women, who do not pay my salary and who have no physical or political or organizational clout over me, but who have my utmost respect; and if their combined wisdom advised me to take a long walk off a short pier, I'd walk.

If a Christian on the pew disagrees with the elders over a matter of conscience, the elders do not become that person's law. However, in matters of judgment, we should be willing to be led by a plurality of elders who have been chosen by the congregation as leaders because they are the most spiritually mature people in the church. I cannot imagine why I should ever think myself too wise to follow their combined judgment. Something would be wrong with my heart (if not my head) should I choose to go my own way rather than respect the combined wisdom of such shepherds. No. Not because they have "position over me," but because of the force of *moral suasion*.

How Long Does "Authority" Last?

How long does an "appointed" elder remain an elder? The Bible does not answer this question. The two Greek word groupings translated "appoint" in the English Bible send no signals on length of tenure nor is tenure discussed in these texts. Therefore, since it is not discussed in the New Testament, we conclude that elder tenure is left to human discretion and may vary from setting to setting. Churches across the country approach it in a variety of ways—some disastrous, some good, some great.

For example, some congregations rotate a certain percentage of their elders annually by democratic process. This method is not biblical or unbiblical. It is simply one way of doing things. In other congregations, elders appoint additional elders for two-, three-, or four-year tenures. Then when the cycle is repeated, the "incumbent" elders automatically step back. In other churches, the elders come before the church at predetermined intervals, some annually, others at two- to four-year intervals, asking if the church wishes to reaffirm them and asking if the church wishes to appoint additional shepherds.

Most churches, however, seem to favor a long tenure for elders, lending stability to the church and building deeper relationships and trust between flock and shepherds. And in most churches of my fellowship, once a man is appointed, he is expected to be an elder as long as he wants to serve and is genuinely functioning in this role, and as long as he can physically and mentally bear up under the stress—and, of course, as long as he is spiritually and morally qualified. Obviously, this is the important issue of tenure. Since an elder's work depends on the authority of moral suasion, when his life is no longer credible, he can no longer function. In short, the elder's heart and character determine the length of his tenure.

When a Shepherd Gets off the Path

How then should this spiritual and moral "qualification" be determined? Again, a number of congregations operate under a shepherds' agreement that any one elder is accountable to all of the elders together. If one elder needs admonishing, correcting, or even removal from his role, the rest of the elders are to see to that. However, if an individual member of a congregation believes that he or she genuinely sees ethical, moral, or spiritual failure in an elder, the Bible outlines clear action steps for that person. That person should approach the situation in the same way he or she would confront any offending Christian.

First, he or she should approach that elder privately. This is Jesus' direct teaching on gentle, loving confrontation.[3] If that elder ignores this private process, he or she should take along two or three witnesses and try again.[4] And if those two steps fail, "tell it to the church."[5] I assume this means, "Have the whole church confront him." Imagine the corrective power if five hundred church members, by threes and fours, confronted a faltering elder.

Paul carries Jesus' teaching directly into relationships with elders. First Timothy 5:19 says, "Do not entertain an accusation against an elder unless it is brought by two or three witnesses." By implication, if three or four people see an elder sin blatantly enough that all of them can clearly "bear witness," they share the responsibility to do something about it.

> ■
>
> Since it is not discussed in the New Testament, we conclude that elder tenure is left to human discretion.
>
> ■

Paul continues, if the three or four people confront the straying shepherd, but he continues to stonewall the aggrieved sheep, "those who sin are to be rebuked publicly, so that the others may take warning."[6] The "public," before which the rebuke is to take place, *may* be the whole church, but this writer thinks it refers to all the elders: that is, bring the concern to the plurality of shepherds. And "the others" who get "warned" are the other elders. This keeps everybody honest, everything out on the table, without spreading gossip or drawing the entire congregation into a fiasco that could not only hurt the church, but permanently damage the brother who is at fault.

Note that Paul includes two *controlling cautions:* this should be done "without partiality" and only with the collaboration of two or three witnesses.[7] In other words, if you definitely know of something that is significant enough to spiritually disqualify *any* elder, take with you those witnesses who confirm your factual information and go to the individual elder under question. If he will not respond, then take the witnesses with you to the rest of the elders and there, "before all," speak that concern. The elders, then, will be in a position to deal with the validity and seriousness of the charges and take appropriate measures. Other than through this procedure, charges against elders should never be spoken. Period! In fact, Paul says, one should not even *listen* to unsubstantiated charges against elders—"do not *entertain* an accusation."[8]

We conclude, then, that since Scripture does not spell out the tenure of an elder, his work should last as long as his moral suasion remains intact and as long as age, health, and spiritual qualities allow him to function in that shepherding, mentoring, equipping role.

Good Shepherds Shepherd Even After They're Gone

In reality—while an elder may resign from the "counsel of elders" or retire from "the leadership of the church"—there is a sense in which a good shepherd never ceases to shepherd. And when a true shepherd resigns, moves away, or dies, a church will naturally go through a period of disequilibrium. There will be at least some sheep among the flock who, for a time, have no voice to follow.

The Preston Road Church in Dallas, where I ministered for over five years, still feels the long shadow of Robert Bell who passed away nearly two decades ago. Brother Bell was a very successful and respected Texas business man and a long-time elder. During his era, church leadership styles were much more authoritarian than today, and friends who knew and loved him say he was a true "son of his times." But he was a hands-on shepherd. He prayed beside hospital beds, he stood often in the baptistery, and he opened the Word and human hearts in the Bible classroom. Jimmie Gomez, my oldest son's mother-in-law (and cograndparent with Carolyn and me) was a child, then a teen in the Preston Road Church during Robert Bell's active days. She recalls that when she experienced an extended illness, how special it made her feel that "Brother Bell" came frequently to her hospital bedside.

Jimmie remembers "Brother Bell's" lengthy discussions with her, over an open Bible, about her relationship with Christ, and she remembers that Robert Bell baptized her with his own hands. She is one among hundreds.

The Bell's home was filled with table guests and church parties, month after month, for years. They nurtured the growing and helped the weak. At their own expense, the Bells visited missionaries supported by the Preston Road Church. Even though he went to heaven years ago, to this day, Robert Bell's presence is felt in our church—even by those of us who never knew him. The few remaining sheep of the flock he shepherded directly still feel his loss deeply. They not only felt grief over his death, but some still feel like lonely sheep in search of a shepherd. At least one lady shows up every Sunday to greet guests in the lobby, because some forty years ago, Robert Bell groomed her for that task and delegated her that responsibility. She is still responding to the voice of her long-deceased shepherd.

My own father served as an elder for some thirty years. Though afforded little formal education, Dad read voraciously, especially from the Bible, and was gifted as a shepherd because of his approachability and his warm people skills. He also was regarded in his congregation—and far beyond—as a man of considerable spiritual wisdom. As my mother's health deteriorated and Dad's own stamina diminished, he resigned his place in the "council of elders." That relieved him of the stress of meetings, administration, budgets, and the like—for which he had little heart to begin with. But his resignation did not stop his flock from seeking his shepherding. Years after his "resignation," virtually until the time of his death, people of all ages and from all walks of life still came to his door for council, prayer, and wisdom. Even when he lay dying and was unable to speak, a steady stream of people passed by his bed. One minister, with whom Dad had walked through some very painful times, came often to see him in his final days. He stood in the hall outside my father's death room and confided to me, "I come here because I get a blessing just being in the room with him."

"Brother Fletcher" was another shepherd whose life impacted mine tremendously. W. L. Fletcher and I shared birthdays, and for years, we also shared birthday parties. But when he turned eighty the day I turned forty, he was a bit offended at the huge sign on the church marquee that spelled out his age to the whole city! W. L. walked me through many doorways of ministry. When he "retired" as elder, I told him—and felt compelled to tell the whole church—"You may have resigned as an elder of this congregation, but you are still my shepherd. I will continue to look to you for tender shepherding." And I did—as long as he lingered in the land of the living. I am sure I was among hundreds who felt the same.

These are just some of the tender shepherds who will always walk the trails with me. In some ways, I will always feel the touch of these shepherds' hands on my life and hear the call of their voices. They will always have great authority in my life.

No question about it: Good shepherds wield tremendous authority. Thank you, Lord.

A Stroll into the Morning

By the time you reach these final pages, I pray that you feel rising waves of *hope*—hope for a new day for leaders who sense that nothing could be more significant and fulfilling than building people and that nothing could be more thrilling than leading God's church effectively into the twenty-first century. And I pray hope for those who accept the calling to lead, that their journey be joyful and fruitful as they rediscover *shepherding, mentoring,* and *equipping.*

Being a godly shepherd does not require special looks, brains, or talent; in fact, God is depending on ordinary people like you and me to step into his "doable" models of shepherding, mentoring, and equipping. And as we follow Jesus' style of ministry, we will find that not only are lives changed, but life's relationships are greatly enriched.

As John Killinger describes it,

> Turning sheep into shepherds is not very hard when you think of it this way. It is loving them until they are ready to share the love too—until they can't help sharing it because it is filling their lives and running over and has to go somewhere. . . . They finally let go and join the irresistible movement of love. It was like a small flood they couldn't fight anymore, so they relaxed and flowed with it, and now they have a good time loving other people. Eventually the other people will be shepherds too. That's the way it works. We will all be shepherds to one another, sharing the love.[1]

Shepherding, mentoring, and equipping fit who we are. These leadership models are about people, and we are about people. We go to malls to watch people. We read novels because they get inside the psyches of other people. We slap down hard-earned money at the theater to sit in the dark and watch shadow pictures of imaginary people. And we are like this because we are created in the image of God. And people matter to God—above *everything*.

That is why the deep and lasting relationships of authentic spiritual leadership do not work among worldly people. They are only possible among people who know God. Worldly leadership is about power and control and is driven by self-interest. But Jesus says, "Do not be like them. If you want to keep your life, give it away. Deny yourselves. Be servants. The way up is down." Jesus made us into "new creatures," [2] and we no longer see people from a worldly point of view. Once we used people; now we love them.

Then we competed; now we build. Then we controlled; now we serve.

This does not come naturally, however. Left to our own devices, we are virtually incapable of sustaining this kind of love. This love is "the fruit of the Spirit."[3] God pours "his love into our hearts by the Holy Spirit, whom he has given us."[4]

Robyn Davidson roamed for months with a tribe of pastoralists in northwest India.[5] They are called the Rabari or "those outside the way." She writes of her experience in *National Geographic*.

> I would travel around the arid regions of Rajasthan, until I found a group of Rabari with whom I felt a strong rapport. Then I would buy myself a camel or two, live with the Rabari in their village and leave with them on migration. The land where they wandered stretches flat to the horizon. Tarpaulins shade them from the poisonous sun, but not from the baking winds.

Davidson's wanderings in this strange and alien land led her to see life through the eyes of the Rabari. "As the sky lightens, we gather at the fires for tea," she relates. "Again I could hear the shepherds call to their flocks." Those haunting voices followed her like strange, sweet music throughout her travels with the Rabari.

> Each shepherd has slightly different calls, variations on a theme. There are morning calls to move out, a call to bring the sheep to water, and so on. Each man knows his own sheep and vice versa, and his particular flock will disentangle itself from the larger flock and move out behind him into the morning.

How like our journey. Like those sheep, we are among strangers in a foreign and hostile land. We need shepherds. Without them, we perish. So the first question for aspiring spiritual leaders is not, "Am I a shepherd?" but "Am I a sheep?" In this strange and hostile land, do I walk my days under the loving care of a shepherd? And if we listen with the right ears, one voice rings out above all the rest. We are part of his flock and no other. So we disentangle ourselves from all the others and move out behind him into the morning.

Discussion
Questions

Chapter 1. *Shepherds on the Hills of Bible History*

1. Since "shepherd" is such an outdated model, why is it important that we spend time on it?

2. Why is *relationship* so important in the shepherding process? What happens when shepherds try to lead sheep they have no relationship with?

3. What does the author mean by "A shepherd is someone who has a flock"? What happens when a "leader," who has no flock, tries to lead?

4. Share an example of a shepherd you know who leads by relationship. Tell of a specific incident.

Chapter 2. *Distorted Leadership Models*

1. What do you think has caused the distorted perceptions of leadership evidenced in churches today?

2. What appears to be the philosophies and motivations behind (1) the cowboy, (2) the sheriff, and (3) the CEO?

3. Why don't these leadership styles meet the shepherding needs of the flock?

4. How can shepherds break the traditions of distorted models of leadership?

Chapter 3. *Fast-Lane Flocks and Cyber-World Shepherds*

1. What aspects of our fast-lane cyber-world produce challenges for today's shepherds?

2. Agree or disagree: Leaders in contemporary churches can be just as effective at shepherding as those in first-century churches. Why or why not?

3. What example of shepherding in this chapter was most impressive to you? Why?

4. Share an example of fast-lane shepherding that you know of personally.

Chapter 4. *Those Who Have Walked a Long Time in the Same Direction*

1. What evidence exists today that our society is suffering from a lack of mentors? How can this suffering be addressed by shepherds in churches today?

2. What can we learn about mentoring from the example of Jesus? Of the apostles?

3. In Acts 20:17, the Greek word for elders is *presbuteros,* meaning "the older one." What does this word tell us about the traits and role of a mentor?

4. In what ways have you had the opportunity to mentor others?

Chapter 5. *How to Mentor*

1. What makes a person a winsome mentor? What specifically attracts you to a mentor?

2. Share how others have mentored you in (1) showing you how to live, (2) encouraging you to be faithful.

3. Which mentoring story impressed you most in this chapter? What about it impressed you? What did you learn?

4. "Others are being mentored by your walk in the Lord." Explain your reaction to this statement.

Chapter 6. *"Use 'Em or Lose 'Em"*

1. According to Ephesians 4, church leaders are to equip the body for service. Why do you think shepherds sometimes fail to equip their flock?

2. In what ways can shepherds help members be equipped for and assimilated into ministry?

3. Discuss church growth in the following three areas and the important role equipping has in each: (1) numerical growth, (2) spiritual growth, (3) organic growth.

4. How can shepherds determine the gifts of their sheep in order to match them up with appropriate ministries?

5. In what way(s) have you shared your ministry gifts to equip others?

Chapter 7. *How the Chief Shepherd Equipped His Flock*

1. Discuss the concept of equipping at varying levels of "relational intimacy." Why is this concept important?

2. Agree or disagree: "Staff members of the church shall not form their personal friendships from within the congregation." Explain your answer.

3. What steps could be taken to free up your elders to do more shepherding and less managing?

4. What are the advantages of leaders focusing their equipping energies on a small circle of people?

5. How would you respond to a leader who wanted to equip and empower you to do a ministry task?

Chapter 8. *Equipping through the Shared Life*

1. Even though modern-day shepherds cannot spend *all* their time with their flock like Jesus did, what about his style of equipping can they imitate?

2. How did Jesus' relationship style differ from the distorted CEO style?

3. Why is it important that shepherds be open with their flock, and what guidelines determine *how* open they should be?

4. Why is it important that shepherds balance their time between "problem" and "possibility" people?

Chapter 9. *Just What Is an Elder?*

1. If you had a serious problem or needed spiritual guidance, who would you go to? Why?

2. Why is the distinction between "qualifications" and "qualities" important? What do these terms have to do with a "checklist" view of the 1 Timothy and Titus passages on elders?

3. Name some qualities that elders in your congregation might need to have that would be different from the qualities that elders in another congregation might need.

4. What three New Testament words are used to describe elders? Discuss the different emphases of the three words.

5. What does it mean that "elders raise the bar"? Do you think it fair to expect elders to do this? Why?

Chapter 10. *Men of Experience*

1. Why is it important that elders have "been around a long while"? What kinds of things are learned through life experience that help an elder lead others?

2. What is meant by teaching the Word "positively" and "negatively"? On what occasions might an elder need to teach "negatively"?

3. What does the phrase "one-woman man" say about a man besides the fact that he has only one wife?

4. Why is it so important that an elder be a "covenant keeper"?

5. Why are children and parenting issues important in determining a man's ability to be an elder?

6. How does an elder's level of hospitality affect his shepherding?

Chapter 11. *Men of Character*

1. Finish this sentence: An elder must be *consistently* _____ and _____. Why is this type of consistency important?

2. Over what does an elder need to exercise "negative" *self-control?* Why is his leadership hampered if he does not control himself in these areas?

3. Discuss examples of when an elder would need to make decisions based on *conviction* rather than *pragmatism.*

Chapter 12. *Men of Vision*

1. How can an elder encourage "reluctant" sheep to move ahead?

2. What are some of the special issues that contemporary, pluralistic churches have to deal with? What issues is your church dealing with that require "flexible leadership"?

3. Why do some people in our society "church shop"? What kind of church is most likely to make "shoppers" want to stay?

4. Discuss the advantages and disadvantages of having numerous elders and, thus, a smaller sheep-to-shepherd ratio.

5. What is the difference between "shepherding" and "administrating"? What "administration" tasks could be delegated to people other than elders? Why are elders sometimes reluctant to delegate?

6. Agree or disagree: "Elders are obligated to try to please *everyone.*" Discuss your answer.

Chapter 13. *The Biblical Language of "Authority"*

1. How does the biblical definition of the word "bishop" differ from common contemporary concepts of this word?

2. How does the word "rule" in the King James Version distort the biblical idea intended?

3. Who is 1 Thessalonians 5:13 referring to when it says "those who rule over you"? Are Christians obligated to "obey" an elder just because he "said so"? Why or why not?

4. What phrases or words in the list of words that "won't break bones" are especially appealing to you? Why?

5. What did you learn in this chapter about the "authority" of elders?

Chapter 14. *The Authority of Moral Suasion*

1. What does the author mean by "moral suasion"? How is this different from "asserting authority"?

2. What determines how long an elder should remain an elder?

3. If an elder "gets off the path," how should he be confronted? If he doesn't respond to the first efforts, then what?

4. What does it mean that "A true shepherd shepherds even after he's gone"?

Additional Resources

Lucado, Max. 1995. *Wanted: A Few Good Shepherds: A Biblical Study of Church Leadership*. Dallas: Word Publishing.

Strauch, Alexander. 1988. *Biblical Eldership: An Urgent Call to Restore Biblical Church Leadership*. Littleton, Colo.: Lewis and Roth Publishers.

Waller, Ted H. 1991. *With the Sheep in the Wilderness: Shepherding God's Flock in the World*. Nashville: Twentieth Century Publishers.

N O T E S

Chapter 1. Shepherds on the Hills of Bible History

1. Ted H. Waller, *With the Sheep in the Wilderness: Shepherding God's Flock in the World* (Nashville: Twentieth Century Publishers, 1991), 9–10.

2. Ps. 23:1.

3. Isa. 40:11.

4. Ps. 100:3; Ezek. 34:31.

5. Isa. 53:6.

6. 1 Sam. 13:14.

7. Ps. 78:70–72.

8. Jer. 50:6.

9. Ezek. 34:2, 4–5.

10. Jer. 25:34.

11. Ezek. 34:23–24.

12. Luke 15:5–6.

13. John 10: 27, 5.
14. John 10:3–5.
15. 1 Pet. 5:4.
16. John 21:15.
17. John 21:16.
18. John 21:17.
19. John 17:18.
20. Acts 20:28.
21. 1 Pet. 5:2–4.
22. John 10:7.
23. John 10:9.
24. John 10:11.
25. Mark 3:14.
26. John 10:4.
27. Matt. 28:20.
28. John 10:3.
29. Ibid.

Chapter 2. Distorted Leadership Models

1. John 10:12.
2. Ps. 23:4.
3. Matt. 16:24.
4. Matt. 20:25–26.
5. John 10:5.

Chapter 4. Those Who Have Walked a Long Time in the Same Direction

1. *American Heritage Dictionary* (Boston: Houghton Mifflin Co.), 821.

2. *Webster's New Collegiate Dictionary* (Springfield, Mass.: Merriam, 1953).

3. Robert Bligh, *Iron John* (New York: Addison-Wesley), 86.

4. Matt. 20:25–28.

5. Matt. 16:24.

6. 1 Cor. 11:1.

7. Phil. 4:9.

8. 2 Thess. 3:6–7.

9. 2 Thess. 3:9.

10. 1 Pet. 5:3.

11. Acts 20:18.

12. Acts 20:35.

13. Acts 20:17.

14. Acts 20:28.

15. 1 Thess. 5:14.

16. 1 Pet. 5:2–3.

17. Eph. 4:11–12.

Chapter 5. How to Mentor

1. *Merriam Webster's Collegiate Dictionary* (Springfield, Mass.: Merriam Webster, Inc., 1994).

2. 2 Cor. 4:16; 5:1; 5:6.

3. Rom. 8:22–25.

4. Heb. 4:15.

5. 1 Cor. 15:58 KJV.

Chapter 6. "Use 'Em or Lose 'Em"

1. Eph. 4:7, 11.

2. Eph. 4:12.

3. See Rom. 12:1–10.

4. Eph. 4:12.

5. Matt. 28:18–20; Mark 16:16; Acts 2:41, 47; 6:1–7.

6. Eph. 4:14.

7. Eph. 4:13. See also John 15:1–8; James 1:22–23; 2 Pet. 1:5–8.
8. Eph. 4:16. See also Rom. 12:1–10; Eph. 4:1–14; Phil. 2:1–5.
9. Eph. 4:16.
10. Rom. 12:6–8.
11. 1 Cor. 12:7.
12. 1 Pet. 4:10.
13. Eph. 4:16.
14. 2 Tim. 2:2.

Chapter 7. How the Chief Shepherd Equipped His Flock

1. Matt. 14:13–21; Mark 6:32; Luke 9:10–17; John 6:5–13.
2. See Luke 10:1.
3. Mark 3:14.
4. Matt. 17.
5. Matt. 26:36–46; Mark 14:32–42; Luke 22:39–46.
6. John 13:23.
7. Eph. 4:16.
8. John 4:34.
9. John 9:4.
10. John 17:4.
11. John 17:18.
12. 2 Tim. 2:2.

Chapter 8. Equipping through the Shared Life

1. John 15:14–15.
2. John 13:1.
3. John 13:23.
4. Mark 11:15–17.
5. Max Lucado, *No Wonder They Call Him the Savior* (n.p.: Multnomah Press, 1986).
6. Heb. 4:15.

7. 1 Pet. 2:21–23.
8. John 13:1–5.
9. John 13:12, 14–17.
10. Eph. 4:11–13 RSV.
11. John 10:10.

Chapter 9. Just What Is an Elder?

1. Acts 20:17, 28.

2. Carl R. Holladay, "The Leadership of the Elders: Its Nature and Extent" paper presented to Dr. J. W. Roberts, in partial fulfillment of the requirements for the course "Advanced Greek Readings," Greek 5382, Abilene Christian College, May 20, 1969.

3. H. W. Beyer, *"episkopos,"* *Theological Dictionary of the New Testament* (ed. Gerhard Kittel; trans. G. W. Bromiley; 5 vols.; Grand Rapids: Eerdmans, 1966), 2:617.

4. 1 Tim. 3:1–7.

5. Titus 1:6–9.

6. Diogenes Laertius (7:116–16) as quoted by William Barclay, *The Daily Bible Study Series;* The Letters to Timothy, Titus and Philemon (Philadelphia: The Westminster Press, 1960), 86–87.

7. Ibid.

8. Titus 1:9.

9. Titus 1:10–11.

10. Max Lucado, *Wanted: A Few Good Shepherds: A Biblical Study of Church Leadership* (Dallas: Word Publishing, 1995), 19.

Chapter 10. Men of Experience

1. 1 Tim. 3:6 KJV, NASB.
2. 1 Tim. 5:22.
3. 1 Tim. 3:2.
4. Eph. 4:11.

5. Titus 1:9.

6. Ibid.

7. Titus 2:1, 3–4, 6.

8. Titus 1:9.

9. Titus 1:6; 1 Tim. 3:2.

10. 2 Pet. 2:14.

11. 1 Tim. 3:11. Of course, this verse comes after a discussion of deacons, and thus may describe qualities of a "deaconess." However, it appears likely to me that when Paul says "their wives" he refers to the wives of both deacons and elders.

12. Titus 1:6.

13. Ibid.

14. 1 Tim. 3:5.

15. Heb. 13:17.

16. 1 Tim. 3:3; 1 Pet. 5:3.

17. Luke 15:5.

18. Luke 15:7.

19. 1 Tim. 3:2; Titus 1:8.

Chapter 11. Men of Character

1. 1 Tim. 3:2.

2. 1 Tim. 3:7.

3. Luke 16:8.

4. Titus 1:7.

5. 1 Tim. 3:3.

6. Carl Spain, *The Letters of Paul to Timothy and Titus* (Austin, Tex.: Sweet, 1970), 59.

7. 1 Tim. 3:3; Titus 1:7.

8. Spain, *Letters to Timothy and Titus*.

9. Rom. 14:21.

10. Phil. 2:4.

11. Gal. 5:13.

12. 1 Tim. 3:2.

13. Titus 1:8.

14. 1 Tim. 3:2.

15. Titus 1:9.

16. Titus 1:10–11.

17. Ps. 78:71–72.

18. Ps. 139:23–24.

Chapter 12. Men of Vision

1. Lucado, *Wanted: A Few Good Shepherds,* 5.

2. See Acts 6.

3. 1 Cor. 4:1.

4. 1 Cor. 4:4–5.

5. John 5:44 RSV.

Chapter 13. The Biblical Language of "Authority"

1. Acts 20:28; Phil. 1:1; 1 Tim. 3:2; Titus 1:7 KJV.

2. Holladay, "The Leadership of the Elders."

3. This discussion of *episkopos* leans heavily on the work of Dr. Carl Holladay, and on the article by H. W. Beyer in *The Theological Dictionary of the New Testament.*

4. Beyer, 602.

5. Judg. 15:1; 2 Chron. 34:12.

6. Jer. 23:2; Ezek. 34:11–12.

7. Zech. 11:16 RSV.

8. James 1:27.

9. Phil. 2:2–5.

10. Holladay, 17.

11. Acts 6:3 KJV.

12. Holladay, 17.

13. Acts 20:28; 1 Pet. 5:3; John 10.

14. 1 Pet. 5:3.

15. 1 Tim. 5:17 RSV.

16. Henry George Liddel and Robert Scott, *A Greek-English Lexicon* (New York: Harper & Brothers, 1883), 1285.

17. 2 Sam. 13:17 RSV.

18. 1 Chron. 27:31 RSV.

19. 2 Chron. 8:10.

20. J. N. D. Kelly, *A Commentary on the Pastoral Epistles* (London: Adam and Charles Black, 1963), 124; Donald Guthrie, *The Pastoral Epistles* (London: The Tyndale Press, 1967), 105; J. H. Thayer, *Greek-English Lexicon of the New Testament* (Grand Rapids: Zondervan, 1962), 539.

21. Bo Riecke, *"Proisteemi," Theologisches Worterbuch zum Neuen Testament* (ed. G. Kittel; Stuttgart: W. Kohlhanmmer, 1959), 6:700.

22. 1 Tim. 3:12.

23. Eph. 6:1–4.

24. Luke 10:35.

25. 1 Thess. 5:12–13.

26. 1 Thess. 5:12.

27. Acts 20:17–21; 1 Thess. 2:9; 3:10; 2 Thess. 3:8.

28. 1 Thess. 5:12.

29. William Neil, *The Epistle of Paul to the Thessalonians* (London: Hodder and Stoughton, 1965), 122.

30. Phil. 2:29.

31. 1 Cor. 16:16.

32. James Hope Moulton and George Milligan, *The Vocabulary of the Greek Testament* (Grand Rapids: Eerdmans, 1949), 541 and F. J. A. Hort, *The Christian Ecclesia* (London: Macmillan and Co., 1897), 126.

33. 1 Thess. 5:12.

34. Rom. 15:14; 1 Cor. 4:14; Col. 1:28.

35. J. E. Frame, *A Critical and Exegetical Commentary on the Epistles of St. Paul to the Thessalonians* (Edinburgh: T. & T. Clark, 1965), 194.

36. 1 Thess. 5:13.

37. Friedrich Buchsel, *"Eegeomai," Theological Dictionary of the New Testament* (ed. G. Kittel; trans. G. W. Bromiley; Grand Rapids: Eerdmans, 1966), 907.

38. Luke 22:25–26.

39. Acts 7:10 RSV.

40. Acts 14:12.

41. Acts 15:22.

42. Luke 22:25–26.

43. Heb. 13:17.

44. 1 Cor. 16:16.

45. Eph. 5:21; Phil. 2:1–4.

46. Matt. 28:18.

47. Acts 20:28–29.

48. 1 Tim. 3:5.

49. 1 Tim. 5:17; Eph. 4:11.

50. Titus 1.

51. James 5:14.

52. 1 Pet. 5:1–4.

53. Eph. 4:11–14.

Chapter 14. The Authority of Moral Suasion

1. Mark 10:45; Eph. 5:21; Phil. 2:2–9.

2. John 10:9.

3. Matt. 18:15.

4. Matt. 18:16.

5. Matt. 18:17.

6. 1 Tim. 5:20.

7. 1 Tim. 5:21, 19.

8. 1 Tim. 5:19.

Epilogue. A Stroll into the Morning

1. John Killinger, *The Tender Shepherd: A Practical Guide for Today's Pastor* (Nashville: Abingdon Press, 1985), 199.

2. 2 Cor. 5:17.

3. Gal. 5:22.

4. Rom. 5:5.

5. Robyn Davidson, "Wandering with India's Rabari," *National Geographic,* Sept., 1993.